D0971615

Praise for
Real Leadership

"This powerful, practical book is loaded with great ideas to help you achieve better results, faster, in any organization."
—Brian Tracy, author of *How the Best Leaders Lead*

"John's nine simple practices are straightforward and backed by real-life experience. His words will motivate you to lead and live with courage, honor, and integrity."
—David Bach, author of the number one *New York Times* bestselling books *The Automatic Millionaire* and *Start Late, Finish Rich*

"A proven leader in the competitive world of financial services, John Addison knows how to build a great company. His new book is a fascinating and deeply personal account of three decades of success facing challenges and surmounting obstacles, filled with powerful anecdotes and inspiration from great leaders from the past."
—Lee Pollock, Executive Director, The Churchill Centre

"John Addison is one of the greatest businessmen, speakers, and leaders of this generation. Not only has he pulled himself up by his bootstraps and achieved so much in his own business career, but he has selflessly devoted his time and energy to helping thousands of other people be more successful in their own lives. In this book he shares nine practical lessons that everyone, in any career or stage of life, can apply to be a more effective leader."
—Fran Tarkenton, NFL Hall of Fame Quarterback and CEO of Tarkenton Companies

"Reading this book is like having John as your own personal leadership coach. The relatable stories and impactful practices in *Real Leadership* will motivate anyone who is leading a team. This book is just what anyone striving for greatness needs!"

—Don Yaeger, *New York Times* bestselling author

"Many people write and talk about leadership, few of which have demonstrated it, with extraordinary success, like John Addison has. If you want to learn real leadership, then read this book."

—Darren Hardy, CEO Mentor, *New York Times* bestselling author, and former publisher of SUCCESS

"Some people talk about leadership, John Addison eats, drinks, and sleeps it! This book will give you purpose and a plan to lead the life you were meant to live."

—Jeffrey Hayzlett, Primetime TV and Radio Host, Chairman C-Suite Network

"It takes more than a great business model for a company to be successful over the long term. At Baron Capital, we pride ourselves on discovering innovative leaders who can thrive in an always changing business environment. We found that leader in John Addison whose differentiated approach and execution through uncertain financial times resulted in Primerica being a top tier corporation. We would not have made the investment nor would the company have been as successful if not for John's leadership."

—Ron Baron, Chairman and CEO Baron Capital

"*Real Leadership* is a fascinating, stimulating, disarmingly candid, yet profoundly impactful book. John's unique storytelling style makes his powerful points even more penetrating. Leadership is a vital 'life force' that every human being needs to master for every facet of their life and career. This book shows instead of merely telling. You will benefit from reading and living John's advice."

—Jay Abraham, world renowned business growth expert

"John lives and breathes *Real Leadership*. I'm proud to say I witnessed the stories and practices in this book firsthand. He led, he fought, and he served our team. Primerica wouldn't be the company it is today without his leadership. Follow John's simple practices to impact your team and produce *real* results."

—Glenn Williams, CEO Primerica

"John Addison is more than a leader, he's a coach and a motivator. If you want to lead your team and inspire others to great results like John has, *Real Leadership* is the book for you."

—Jack Canfield, the *New York Times* bestselling author of *The Success Principles* and the Chicken Soup for the Soul Series

"True leaders inspire others to lead. John Addison is that kind of leader, inspiring the next generation of leaders using ageless wisdom, modern examples, and practical tools. Positive leadership is practiced, not inherited. And *Real Leadership* lights the way."

—Shawn Achor, the *New York Times* bestselling author of *The Happiness Advantage*

"A must-read for those seeking to improve their leadership skills, manage people or situations better, or simply have a better perspective in life. As John's colleague of 30 years and co-CEO of Primerica for 15 years in both the best and worst of times, I have seen his leadership principles in action. They work—pure and simple."
—**Rick Williams,** former Co-CEO Primerica

REAL
LEADERSHIP

9 SIMPLE PRACTICES FOR LEADING AND LIVING WITH PURPOSE

JOHN ADDISON
WITH JOHN DAVID MANN

Published in partnership with
SUCCESS

Mc
Graw
Hill
Education

New York   Chicago   San Francisco   Athens   London   Madrid
Mexico City   Milan   New Delhi   Singapore   Sydney   Toronto

1 2 3 4 5 6 7 8 9 0   DOC/DOC   1 2 1 0 9 8 7 6

ISBN   978-1-259-58444-2
MHID   1-259-58444-5

e-ISBN 978-1-259-58445-9
e-MHID   1-259-58445-3

Library of Congress Cataloging-in-Publication Data

Addison, John A.
Real Leadership: 9 simple practices for leading and living with purpose /
    John Addison.
New York : McGraw-Hill, [2016]
LCCN 2015038163| ISBN 9781259584442 (alk. paper) | ISBN 1259584445
    (alk. paper)
LCSH: Addison, John A. | Success in business. | Leadership. | Success. |
    Conduct of life.
LCC HF5386 .A5144 2016 | DDC 658.4/092—dc23 LC record available at
    http://lccn.loc.gov/2015038163

Contents

Foreword

....

If you are reading this foreword, "Congratulations!" You have in your possession, a life-altering vehicle. If you internalize the contents that follow and apply the lessons learned with honest commitment, the timely and timeless wisdom offered will give you the change only a few readers experience through the pages of a single book.

Having devoted my career to studying leaders and winners in every walk of life, I consider it a privilege to add a few opening comments about John Addison's extraordinary masterpiece. To write about leadership with authenticity and credibility, the author, of necessity, must exemplify—by his own actions—the critical traits that define true leadership. John Addison has lived the principles he shares with us in his unique, inimitable "homespun" style. His warmth, humility, stewardship attitude and lack of hubris are legendary among all those, like myself, who have come to know his core values over a long period of time. Pure and simple, John "walks his talk." He is the real thing, *sine cera*, without wax.

It is one thing to write a glowing, one-line testimonial about a colleague's new book. It is another thing, entirely, to attempt to do justice to great book in the foreword. I realize that many eager readers skip the foreword and go straight to Chapter One. (I do that often, myself.) But if you are reading this, here is what makes this work one that only surfaces once in every decade, if that often:

It has been said that "the greatest teachers are themselves the greatest students," and I can say, emphatically, that John is a lifelong student of what differentiates an empowering, inspiring leader from the command and control leader of the past. There are several major differences that make this book so relevant and special.

First, you must read and re-read the Prologue. It is the essence of the message. Print it and share it with everyone in your sphere of influence. The five lines that define John's philosophy of living a life of purpose should be mailed or texted to everyone in the world with a smart-phone.

I don't like to make comparisons, but, in this case, I feel compelled. This book, *Real Leadership: 9 Simple Practices for Leading and Living with Purpose* is as impactful as my late friend Stephen Covey's global blockbuster *The 7 Habits of Highly Effective People*. What excites me about *Real Leadership*, is that it is the story of a common man who becomes uncommonly successful by focusing on solutions to the problems we all face and by bringing out the best in everyone he encounters, which he refers to as "shining your light on others." It is not about leadership theory as taught in Ivy League schools or in think tanks. It resonates with us, the readers, who are trying hard to believe that "things turn out best for those who make the best of the way things turn out."

Each of the nine (9) simple practices, that are featured in the nine chapters, is a priceless gem in its own right. Together they remind me of a present-day, easily understandable version of the classic essays of Ralph Waldo Emerson, one of my favorite philosophers. Addison encourages us to seriously engage in the action steps at the end of each chapter. While action steps are common to many self-help books in recent generations, I believe these are believable and achievable if we make the effort to convert these actions into a conscious, daily regimen. As every Olympian I have trained has discovered, practice makes permanent. No train, no gain.

I have been up close and personal in observing John Addison's incredible journey for nearly thirty years. I consider him a colleague worth emulating and a lifelong friend. When you read this book, you will understand why.

Denis Waitley, author
The Psychology of Success and *The Psychology of Winning*

Acknowledgments

I'd like to say a heartfelt thank you to my parents, John and Ruth Addison, two of the greatest parents anyone could have. They gave me roots and wings not loot and things.

To my family, Loveanne, Kyle, and Tyler: God truly blessed me with a wonderful wife and the two best boys (now men) in the world. You have made me a blessed man.

To my business partner Rick Williams, my dearest friend and the greatest business partner anyone could ever have. You and I fought the fights, won the battles, and did something amazing together.

To my friend Glenn Williams, and the leaders and people of Primerica: You have impacted and changed my life more than anything I ever did for you. It was the honor of my life to serve you and our cause.

To my friends: I am truly a wealthy man because I have a wealth of wonderful friends who enrich my life every day.

To John David Mann and Amy Anderson: You guys captured my voice to make this book possible.

To Stuart Johnson and the SUCCESS team: Thank you for everything you've done. I love you guys.

To Dayna Stuckey, my Radar O'Reilly, thank you for everything you do to make my life work. By the way, what am I supposed to do today?

Prologue

If you were asked to identify the most precious resource in the world, what would you say? I know what my answer would be: *leadership*.

I believe leadership is the single most valuable, most important commodity there is—and the scarcest. Not oil, not land, not cash, not technological know-how, but tenacious, focused leadership. Leadership is everything.

There are many different styles of leadership. One of the most colorful leaders of World War II, with his brilliance and his ivory-handled revolvers and his ego bigger than a Sherman tank, was George Patton. Patton certainly got results. But I lean toward being more of an Omar Bradley kind of guy. General Bradley spoke quietly and wore a uniform so plain he was occasionally mistaken for a private. They called Bradley "the G.I.'s general." He commanded 1.3 million men—the largest body of American soldiers ever to serve under a U.S. field commander, and he did a tremendously good job.

There's no doubt that an autocratic, carry-a-big-stick leadership style—the kind that works through fear and intimidation—can be effective. However, if you want to be a leader for the long term, that approach generally doesn't work out too well.

There is a leadership style that fosters not just results but purpose. The kind of real leadership that comes from an authentic concern and respect for those we're leading. The kind of leadership that draws people to follow you even when they may disagree with you because they trust you and know they can count on you.

If you want to lead people in that deeper way, in a way that achieves results without an oppressive game of who's boss, then you have to *inspire* them—inspire them to commit to a cause, to better themselves, to live their truest lives.

So how do you do that?

Well, you could just try to be as impressive as possible, inspiring people by your mere presence. I don't know about you, but that one doesn't work for me. Frankly, I'm just not all that impressive.

When I'm getting ready to go out in front of an audience and talk, there's not really any "getting ready" to it. I put a good deal of thought and preparation into what I want to say. But once it's time to show up, it's pretty much just go out there and talk. I'm not practicing my opening lines. I don't have a makeup artist. I've been in the green room before a lot of events, and sometimes it seems like the level of preparation people can go through is just unreal. With me, hey, how I look is how I look. I'm not thinking about getting my face made up or my hair sprayed into place or getting myself to look perfect. I don't have a speech on a teleprompter all lined out. I go out there with my Georgia accent and my imperfect sentences and my pages of handwritten notes—single words, a few phrases, the bare essence of what I want to get across—and then it's just me and whoever's out there sitting in those seats listening. Whatever I got, that's it. I'm not thinking about how the sizzle sounds; I'm focused on the steak. And it's not like I come out on stage and talk some noble high-flying philosophy and then go backstage and holler at people and throw things. What you see is what you get. I'm real.

The basic facts of my story are these:

At the age of 25, I went to work at a company where I never planned to stay for more than a few years. Over the following three decades, I rose through the ranks, weathering ownership changes and executive leadership changes. Eventually, serving with Rick Williams as co-CEO of Primerica and surrounded by incredible leadership in our sales force out in the field, we took that company through the epicenter of the worst financial collapse in generations. The odds of our emerging intact, whole and healthy, were astronomically small, yet emerge we did, and we have seen our market cap double in the five years since.

> You get up every day and aim to be a little better than you were yesterday.

This book is less a chronicle of exactly how that all happened than it is my attempt to show you *why* that happened. The Nine Practices highlighted in these nine chapters are a systematic breakdown of my approach to leadership, an approach built up over these decades from the examples of exceptional people I've had the good fortune to know. They are my best effort to give you a deconstructed recipe for real leadership.

My view is that you get up every day and aim to be a little better than you were yesterday.

You figure out what you're naturally good at, then focus on building those strengths and don't fuss about the things you're mediocre at. You work hard, try to be a person of generous spirit, and make your success about shining your light on the people around you, not on yourself. You do your best to develop enough likeability in yourself that you'll have people around you who are pulling for you instead of trying to pull you down. And when things get rough, as they will always do, you have the courage to stand firm—and then keep standing firm.

The five sentences you just read sums up what I've done throughout my life and my career.

I'm a normal guy who happened to find himself in abnormal circumstances. That's not false modesty. It's the plain truth. I've worked hard to get where I got, always did well in school (Mom made sure of that) and graduated from college *cum laude*, got my MBA with honors—but from the University of Georgia and Georgia State University, not from Harvard or Stanford. I am not your Ivy League–bred, Wall Street–trained CEO from central casting. When I entered the business world, I was just a kid from an average middle-income family in Georgia. I like to joke that the first time I went into the boardrooms of Manhattan they had to bring in a Southern translator to understand what I was saying.

Let's just say, Gordon Gekko and I don't have all that much in common.

Don't get me wrong. The way things have worked out for me? That was no accident. I've worked my butt off and done my level best to do right by the people I've worked with. All I'm saying is that I haven't achieved what I have because I'm anything special or extraordinary or unique. I've had the great fortune of knowing some good people along the way who've taught me, through their words and even more through their actions, some fundamental leadership principles that have stood me well and steered me straight. These are my own personal laws of success. What they really come down to is *principles of living your best life*.

To me, the essence of real leadership is having the courage to live your true life, the one you were put here to live, and to do it in a way that makes the world a better place than it was before you got here.

We thought about titling this book *Personal Development for the Rest of Us*. Because I'm not going to tell you that to be a success, you have to get up every morning and work out for three hours, and then do your affirmations for another three hours, and then reread your goals list a hundred times, and then go out there and by the end of the day have every one of those goals accomplished and ticked off that list. If that's what it takes to be a successful leader, then let's be honest: Neither one of us stands a chance.

Fortunately for you and me, that's *not* what it takes. You don't have to be some superhuman being to have out-of-the-ordinary success as a leader. Real, purpose-filled leadership is something we can all accomplish. I hope my story will show you that.

So here's the thing. I'm going to tell you my story—but as you read these pages remember that the point is not to tell the story for the story's sake. The point is to offer whatever experiences and perspectives I can in hopes that they may help you work out what *your* story is and muster the courage to live it full out.

Here, as I see it, is the bottom line: When it comes to carving out the life you were put here to live, achieving great success, and being a leader who inspires, there are only two things that really matter.

There's what happens.

And there's what you do about it.

Luck happens. Any truly successful leader who tells you luck had nothing to do with it is a liar. Whether you call it lucky breaks, good fortune, or Divine Providence, the plain truth is that circumstances will happen that are beyond your control and that change the course of your life, sometimes for the worse and sometimes for the better. You can't do a thing about it. It just happens. But that's not the whole story. It's not even the important part of the story. The important part of the story, the only part that honestly matters, is that second thing:

What you do about it.

Lucky breaks come by chance. Success comes by choice.

When people win at roulette, that's luck. When people win at life, it's not luck; it's because they learned how to meet circumstances head on and respond in a way that works—and that works to the highest good. Does it help to be in the right place at the right time? Of course. But that "right place at the right time" shows up a lot more often than you might think. It's not a once-in-a-lifetime thing. In fact, it happens all the time. Most people just don't recognize it or show up to meet it when it does. The world is full of people who happen to be at the right place at the right time. That's not good enough. Winners do the *right things* at the right place at the right time.

> Lucky breaks come by chance. Success comes by choice.

The truth is that you don't have to be brilliant, or exceptionally talented, or unusually lucky to be a leader who makes a powerful and positive difference. The truth is, you can achieve way more than people who are way smarter than you are, way more talented than you are, and even way luckier than you are, just by showing up, taking the right actions, working hard at it, and being an honorable person.

So yes, luck happens. Events shape your life. But there's another truth, too. You can also shape events. Sometimes that takes courage, even a lot of courage. But just remember this: The courage to be yourself, to do the right thing and to devote yourself to making a positive difference in others' lives, is all it takes to change the world. And that's real leadership.

A Note on the Action Steps

At the end of each chapter, you'll find a summary of the "practice" associated with that chapter, and at the end of each summary I've listed a single ACTION STEP you can take to put that practice into operation.

You may have read books before with those lists of things to do, and if you're like most people, you may have said, "Hmm, sounds like a good idea," or, "I'll come back to that later." I want to encourage you to do something different this time.

This time, don't just read them.

This time, actually *do* them.

Real leadership, the kind of leadership that inspires, doesn't spring up all at once, fully formed, out of nowhere. It isn't born in a flurry of thunder and lightning, out of some amazing breakthrough or dramatic event, no matter how much it may seem that way from external appearances. Real leadership emerges over time as an expression of who you are and what you do every day. More than anything, it takes shape as a result of everyday practice.

These nine ACTION STEPS represent the distillation of everything I've experienced, witnessed, and learned in the world of leadership. If you take the time and initiative to actually put them into practice every day, I can make you this promise: They will change your life—and in your own way, in your own time, you will change the world.

First Things First

Decide Who You Are

Be true to yourself. Help others. Make each
day your masterpiece. Drink deeply from good
books. . . . Make friendship a fine art.

—JOHN WOODEN

As a teenager, Benjamin Franklin spent hours studying editions of his brother's newspaper, *The New England Courant*, outlining the essays and then rewriting them in his own words. This was the same kid who as an adult would become the publisher of *Poor Richard's Almanack*, coauthor of the Declaration of Independence, and one of the most famous Americans of his, or any, generation. That was years in the future for the teenaged Ben. He knew his older brother would never allow him to actually write for the *Courant*, so he composed his letters of social commentary in secret and signed them with the pen name "Silence Dogood." Ben snuck them under the front door of the newspaper office at night. A revolutionary man of letters in the making!

Then there was the young Steve Jobs, who was always tinkering with electronics. By the age of 14, he was already talking with Steve Wozniak about building computers together. Or the young Marvin Hamlisch, who at the age of eight told his father, "I want to be the next Cole Porter." Six-time Tony-Award winner Audra MacDonald remembers as a little girl practicing Tony acceptance speeches while proudly holding her hairbrush as a stand-in for the award statuette.

These stories inspire me. I greatly admire people who knew their destiny practically before they could walk. I'm totally impressed when I hear about people who set their feet on the path of life early on with big, bold, ambitious blueprints for their careers.

I am not one of these people.

You hear about men and women who charted out their lives with amazing detail. "I want to be published by age thirty, climb Mount Kilimanjaro by age forty, have dinner at the White House by age 50. . . ." It amazes me when I hear stories like that. Apparently I'm just not wired that way. My approach to life has pretty much been to jump in the river and start swimming. When the river branches off, I just do my best to take the fork that looks like the right one.

Looking at where my life is today, I could never have imagined any of this happening 35 years ago, not under any circumstances. I'm the first to admit, I never had a grand plan for my life or master strategy for winding up in the leadership positions I've been in. The way I've always seen it is, you need to get up every morning, make this day an adventure, and do your best to be better than you were yesterday. Spend too much time fussing and worrying about where you're going to be 20 years from now and you might miss out on what you need to be doing 20 minutes from now.

Besides, I'm not sure life really works that way. Things happen that you can't plan. The future isn't entirely up to you. Big goals are great. I'm all for having a huge dream. There's an awful lot you can't predict nor control. What you *can* control is who you are and how you respond to the challenges that come your way.

If you're wondering about any early autobiographical epiphanies or moments of epic clarity that I may have experienced when I suddenly knew why I was here and what I was supposed to do with my life . . . well, there weren't any. I didn't have a clue.

Actually, that's not quite accurate. Looking back I can see that there *were* plenty of clues and hints along the way. At the time, I didn't know they were clues and hints. My plan, if you can call it *a plan*, was to keep putting one foot in front of the other and live in a way that would make my parents proud.

> What you *can* control is who you are and how you respond to the challenges that come your way.

I'm not saying goals and dreams aren't important. They're incredibly important. There's something even more important—something that comes first. The first 25 years of my life were about getting a solid handle on that *what comes first*.

My First Role Model

Over the years I've had quite a few heroes and role models, among them Benjamin Franklin, Thomas Jefferson, Abraham Lincoln, and especially Winston Churchill. I've had people who've worked with me side by side every day whom I also consider my heroes. I've had bosses from whom I've learned a great deal and I've had people who've worked for me who've taught me just as much. But the person who taught me the most and who I've most sought to emulate throughout my life and my career is my mother.

Ruth Dalton grew up in Moultrie, a farming community in southwest Georgia, with eleven brothers and sisters and practically no money. The Daltons were farmers, scratching out a living off the land as best they could. For whatever reason, Ruth always had a strong independent streak in her character. She read a great deal and was always up on current events. After high school and college, she moved to Atlanta and took a job with the Georgia Department of Labor. There she eventually met a young man named John Addison.

I wish I could go back in time and observe my mom during those Atlanta years, when she was in her twenties. I have photos of her as a young woman. All dressed up, she looked like a movie star. I have a feeling that whenever she walked into a room, all heads turned. She must have just about sucked all the oxygen out of the place.

By the time she met my dad and got married she was already in her thirties. This was fairly unusual at a time when most women married and started families in their twenties. But she put the parties and big-city living firmly behind her and threw herself into family life with everything she had.

Although my father had a good job in Atlanta, where he worked for a textile manufacturing company called Fulton Bag and Cotton Mill, my parents didn't want to raise me there. They'd both grown up in small towns and made a conscious choice to embrace the country life, even if that meant my father had to commute to work. They moved out to Covington, a little city about 35 miles southeast of Atlanta, and settled in a little rural community on the outskirts of Covington called Salem.

To give you a sense of where I grew up, the first five episodes of *The Dukes of Hazzard* were filmed in and around Covington. *My Cousin Vinny* was filmed there, too. Salem is a tiny place, which at the time had a general store, a filling station, a church (Salem Methodist, of which we were members), and not much else. It was a lot like growing up with Andy Taylor in Mayberry, except that it wasn't on television, it was our lives.

I remember going into Covington one day with my mom to do some shopping. This was 1961 or 1962. I would have been four or five years old. I was an only child, and although my mom had worked before I was born and would work again later when I entered junior high school, during those early years she wanted to be a stay-at-home mom. We were together a lot, and I often went on errands with her. On this particular day, when we approached the cash register to pay for our items, there was an African-American woman standing at the end of the short line in front of us.

You have to understand, this was the early sixties. The Civil Rights Movement was still young, and we were living deep in the heart of Georgia. At that time, in that part of the world, if a white person got in line at a store, an African-American person was supposed to step out of the line and let the white person go ahead of them. So it was no surprise, as the two of us stepped up to the line, to hear the checkout girl's voice saying firmly to the woman ahead of us, "Ma'am, you need to step out of line and let this lady in."

What happened next *was* a surprise, both to the checkout girl and to the woman in front of us. My mom immediately reached out to touch the woman on the shoulder and said, "No, no, no—you were ahead of me." And to the checkout girl she added, "I don't want to hear that. We don't do that."

I don't remember the other woman saying a word, but I'll never forget the look on her face. A mix of surprise, gratitude, and something I couldn't put a word to then, but if I'd known the word I might have called *dignity*. I watched that woman pay for her groceries, and as she left the store it seemed to me that she stood at least two inches taller than when she'd come in. Something about that brief exchange with my mom had changed something in her. With just a gesture and a few words, my mom had acknowledged the woman's sense of self-worth and helped it to shine.

As a five-year-old, I couldn't articulate all that or process any of it logically. But I got it. Five-year-olds see and understand a lot more than most people give them credit for. There was something thrilling about what had just happened, something that made me feel so proud of my mom I could have burst—and also made me say, somewhere down inside, "I want to be like *that* when I grow up," even though if you'd asked me then, I couldn't have told you exactly what *that* was.

Look for the Best in People

My parents and I were very close. I can't remember a single argument or fight ever taking place in our home. My dad does have a temper, though, and it can get away from him now and then if he's provoked. I remember times when he'd get upset about something someone had done and go on a rant about the person. Mom would just listen, nodding quietly, not saying a thing—at least not then. The next day, though, or maybe the day after that, the two of them would be sitting talking about some completely different topic, and she would suddenly bring up that person's name and mention something good they'd done. My dad would go quiet. Then she'd look over at him and give him a look. "You need to let that go, John," she'd say. And he would. He knew she was right.

I wish I could say that, growing up in Salem, I always looked for the best in people the way my mother did, but it wouldn't quite be the truth. The best I can say is that it was the target I set for myself. Some of my most vivid childhood memories are of times that I fell short of that target and felt the sting of disappointment—not in others, but in myself.

They had a tradition in my school, where each kid would bring in a Christmas present for another kid in the class. But you didn't get to choose who you were giving your present to.

They would match us up by drawing our names at random from a hat. One year, when I was seven or eight years old, I got paired up with a boy named Gordon.

Gordon came from a family who clearly had no money. I don't remember what he gave me, but I do remember that it was something really small and seemingly inexpensive. It certainly was not very impressive. The other kids started making fun of him and his gift, saying it was cheap. Do you know the honest truth? I joined in with them.

Have you ever done that? Gone along with the crowd, even when you knew in your bones it wasn't the right thing to do? That's what I did that day. It didn't feel good, but I let myself be swept along in the moment and followed the herd.

When I got home from school, I showed my mom what Gordon had given me, and told her how everyone had reacted.

"Now listen, Johnny," she said. "That's probably all his family could afford. For them, that gift was probably more expensive than the present we bought you to give him."

I felt horrible about it. The idea that my actions had made somebody else feel bad, that I'd hurt someone with my carelessness, was something I just couldn't live with.

The next day, I searched Gordon out as soon as I got to school. I went up to him and thanked him for my present and told him how great it was and how much I liked it. My mom hadn't told me to do that. She didn't have to. Sometimes who you are speaks even louder than what you say.

I've never known anyone, then or since, better at not judging people, at turning the other cheek, at letting things go, at not participating in rumors or gossip, at always building people up and never tearing them down, than my mom. She exemplified the spirit of loving thy neighbor as thyself.

Me, I'm a little more wobbly. I try, but the truth is, we are all baskets of insecurities, mistakes, regrets, and other human imperfections. I always admired how my mom would consistently look for the best in others. It took me a while to realize that it's just as important to look for the good in myself, too, and to focus on bringing those qualities out in myself as well as in others.

Leadership starts with leading yourself, which means accepting yourself with all your faults and imperfections, and not beating yourself up when you make mistakes. It also means not letting those dark aspects of yourself control who you *are* in the world, and making the decision to rise above those limitations. If you can do that with yourself, you can do that with others. Accept people's imperfections and be the first to see their good qualities; everyone has them. Be the kind of person others seek out for advice because they trust that you're not going to judge them; you're not going to throw rocks at them; you're not going to tell bad stories about them after you leave.

> Leadership starts with leading yourself.

This is not to say you should be naïve and expect every last person to rise to your good expectations. Let's face it: There are some people in the world whose moral and ethical makeup is just beyond repair. You do need to learn to recognize these folks and to steer clear of them, as much as your situation allows. But you can't let those few toxic people color your view of humanity as a whole. I would rather err by giving a person too many chances than by giving them too few. If I'm going to make a blunder, I'd rather do it in the process of giving someone the benefit of the doubt and trying to help them get ahead, than in holding them back or holding them down.

Will people disappoint you? Sometimes. People do stupid things. We disappoint ourselves; *we* do stupid things. No one's perfect, and I'm a long ways from it. But anyone can make a choice to be a person of honor and character.

It's Not What You Do, It's Who You Are

There's a reason it's so important to have heroes when you're young: That's when you're still deciding who you want to be as you find your way into the life ahead of you. The people you admire most may not necessarily be those whose paths you will follow literally. Having Michael Jordan as a hero doesn't mean your destiny is to be a basketball star, admiring Lincoln doesn't mean you want to be a lawyer or politician. The point of heroes is not necessarily what they *do*. It's who they *are*.

Those early years in Salem taught me that it's worth it to work hard on being someone who delivers on what you say you'll do. Be somebody who people see walking by and think, *there's a man of honor* or *there's a woman of honor*.

In some ways, I *was* lucky. I wasn't born wealthy. I didn't come up through any kind of Ivy League or high-powered business dynasty. I didn't know anything about big-city life and was relatively unsophisticated as to the ways of the world. But I did have very positive and supportive parents who were excellent role models. In baseball terms, let's say, I was born on first base. It wasn't like I had to hit the ball and run to get there. My parents, community, and upbringing gave me that kind of solid head start. I'll always be grateful for that.

I've known people who grew up with wealthy, highly educated parents and all kinds of other advantages. You know the ones I mean: people who were born on third base and think they hit the triple themselves. And I've known people who had a mountain of misfortune to overcome in life—bad background, abusive parents, no money, no advantages—people born swinging at the plate with two strikes already against them.

But all of that is completely beside the point. It's all past; none of us is going to change any of it. You can't change your history. Things that are outside your control are outside your control. Do circumstances matter? It would be naïve to say they don't. Of course, where you're born, where you grow up, who your parents are or aren't, where you're fortunate enough (or unfortunate enough) to go to school, all these circumstances and many others, play a role. But they're not what matters most. What matters most is what you do about it.

You may not be able to map out everything you're going to do in life. But you can decide what you believe in. You can find those things that you know are true, that you know you'll follow no matter what.

> People don't follow what you say. They follow what you do and who you are.

The world of business tends to reveal your character. Sometimes you'll see smart and talented people burst on the scene like a shooting star, and then a few years later you're wondering why you're not hearing about them anymore. You notice everyone saying, "Hey, whatever happened to so-and-so?" I'll tell you what happened to so-and-so. Their character caught up with them. I've seen this scenario replay itself over and over again, more times than I can count. You probably have, too.

Words truly are cheap. Anyone can talk a good line, and a good line may influence people for a time. But not for the long haul. Ultimately people don't follow your words. They follow your integrity, your spirit. They don't follow what you say. They follow what you do and who you are.

No matter who your parents were, where you grew up, what happened to you or didn't, the bottom line is that what kind of person you turn out to be is your decision. I don't mean a decision you make in one big burst of clarity on your eighteenth birthday, in an explosion of light with angels singing. It's a decision you make again and again, every day—in fact, dozens of times a day. We describe ourselves as human beings, but I think the truth is more like this: We are human *becomings*. Being the kind of person others look up to and are glad to be around, the kind of person others will follow, isn't something that happens to you. It's something you decide, something you work on. It's not a gift. It's an ongoing project. And it's more than worth the effort.

When I graduated from Newton High School in 1975 a friend of my dad's gave me a copy of *Great Expectations*. Inside on the flyleaf he had written an inscription: "To Johnny Addison, for whom I have great expectations!"

Well, that made one of us. I sure appreciated the vote of confidence, but as for me, I didn't know what kind of expectations I had. If you'd asked me at the time what were my big goals in life, I probably would have said, "Um . . ." and who knows what would've come out next. The only things I *did* know were who I admired and what kind of behavior I wanted to emulate.

When people know from an early age what they want to do with their lives, I think that's awesome. But I don't believe it's the most crucial thing. I believe what's more crucial than what you do is how you go about doing it. I think what's important is to know what's important. The main thing in life is to know what the main things in life are.

By the time I left for college, I still had absolutely no clue what I wanted to *do*—but I had a pretty good idea of what kind of person I wanted to *be*.

Answer the Call

Joseph Campbell said that every hero's journey starts with answering a "call to adventure." I believe that every one of us is a hero in waiting. Our call to adventure happens every day. At the time, though, you may not realize that's what is happening, because that call may not look as dramatic in real life as it does in the movies. Sometimes it looks like simply taking the next step that's right in front of you.

In the fall of 1975, I left home to go study and live at the University of Georgia (UGA) in Athens. I was not the least bit happy about it.

Mom and Dad had always raised me with the idea that I was going to go to college. I knew that's where I was supposed to be headed, but I honestly did not want to go. Things were great at home. I was happy there. I had a girlfriend who was still in high school. All my friends were there, most of whom were *not* going off to college somewhere. I had no desire to leave the house and make my way in the world. But all that was beside the point. My parents' bottom line was that I was going to college. That was non-negotiable.

So I went. Despite my initial reluctance, I absolutely loved it. College had a huge influence on me. It taught me how to think and gave me an environment where I could read fascinating stuff to my heart's content. I majored in economics and minored in political philosophy, which completely intrigued me. My interest in business had less to do with the nuts, bolts, dollars, and numbers of business itself and more to do with the human behavior of it all. I loved reading history and biographies, and still do to this day. I'd much rather pass a few hours reading about the life of some great statesman than poring over a business book.

As much as I loved my time in college, it didn't exactly clarify what kind of career awaited me. One of my economics professors, a man named Albert Danielson, wrote a letter of recommendation for me that concluded, "I expect Mr. Addison will likely wind up either with a doctorate in economics, or as the CEO of a public company." Dr. Danielson must have seen something I didn't. I graduated from the University of Georgia *cum laude* with a B.A. in economics and not a clue what I was going to do with it.

I spent the next few months living at my parents' home in Salem and commuting into Atlanta every day, looking for work. The U.S. economic conditions weren't great in the fall of 1979, and it certainly was not the best time to be in the job market. Interest rates were through the roof and unemployment was high. I started interviewing for anything and everything I could find. I interviewed with United Airlines to be a reservationist. I interviewed with Atlanta Gaslight to work in their office. I interviewed with Equifax to collect consumer data. It was a completely rudderless experience. Eventually, I landed an entry-level job as an insurance underwriter at a company called Life of Georgia, starting out as a trainee at $207 a week.

The fact was that I was not even the slightest bit interested in the insurance business. What I was interested in was getting an apartment of my own with some of my buddies. I didn't have any particular kind of employment in mind, as long as it was the kind that paid you something. If it would foot my share of the rent and subsidize partying on the weekends, that would do it for me. Insurance underwriting just happened to be what showed up.

Life turns on the smallest of decisions. You never know which ones will prove the most significant.

The moment I had my new job, I went in with two friends on an apartment in a community northeast of downtown, just inside the 285 loop, called Avondale—home to the nation's first Waffle House. The place was a dump. We had a sofa that was so bad it looked like a parody of bad college-dorm furniture. One day we drove by a dumpster and noticed a sofa sitting next to it that someone had thrown away. "That sofa looks better than ours," we said. So we went home, dragged our ratty sofa out to that Dumpster, made the exchange, and brought that other one back to our apartment.

If you had bumped into me at that time, you would not have seen a sign on my forehead reading "Future Chief Executive Officer of a Public Company."

My new employment was a desk job, assessing risks. In other words, I was sitting all day in a chair, looking at pieces of paper. I hated it.

Wait, let me clarify that statement. It wasn't just that I hated it. I hated it *and* I was terrible at it. I can't sit at a desk for twenty minutes, let alone eight hours. Sitting there staring at files, literally all day long except for a lunch break and one other brief break in the afternoon, was sheer torture for me. I was making something like $10,000 a year and doing something I hated and that I wasn't any good at. I did it month after month, throughout 1980. I was learning the meaning of the word *job*.

I believe one of the great keys to a successful life is incremental improvement. It's not about going from where you are today to moving into a mansion with five swimming pools tomorrow. It's not about "quantum leaps" or the big dramatic breakthrough. Those are great for Hollywood films, where the filmmaker has only two hours to get the hero from Point A to Point Z. But back here in reality, where life's major changes and plot points are measured in years rather than minutes, it's about day-by-day personal improvement, finding your path to where it is you want to go, one step at a time. Exciting? No. Dramatic? Hardly. But it does have the advantage of being *real*. Over time it can, indeed, lead to events both dramatic and exciting.

And there's the rub: time.

Incremental improvement doesn't happen automatically, and it sure doesn't happen swiftly. You have to commit to it over a lengthy period of time, and that takes a certain amount of character and spine. A lot of people try to short-circuit the process by jumping around, zigging and zagging through life. They're too impatient, too unfocused, or too willing to follow the next shiny new idea that comes along. Tapping into the great power of incremental improvement takes patience, persistence, and faith. The payoff is well more than worth it.

Throughout 1980 it took every ounce of patience, persistence, and faith I had not to run out of the place screaming.

In 1981, two things happened that showed me it had been worth it to keep plodding along.

Plug into Your *Why*

In early 1981, when I'd been working at Life of Georgia for about a year, they moved me into another department where I was enrolled in a management training program. I don't know if they did this because they saw some sort of potential in me, or if they just took pity on me and knew they had to get this yo-yo out from behind that desk. Whatever the case, I'll be forever grateful that they did it.

> Tapping into the great power of incremental improvement takes patience, persistence, and faith.

For this training program, they brought in a consultant from Paul B. Mulligan and Company, out of Scarsdale, New York. The consultant's name was John Drago, and he changed my life.

John's task was to train a group of us in how to make departments more efficient. I liked him. He was smart and very personable. What's more, this efficiency stuff kind of intrigued me. I couldn't have kept on doing what I'd been doing for too much longer without going crazy or getting fired. I had no passion for the work. My only motivation for showing up every day was paying for my share of the apartment, Dumpster sofa and all.

I liked the work we were doing in John's training. Under his direction, we started doing studies of different departments. Once a study was completed, one of us would have to stand up and present to the senior management our findings. Unlike some of the other folks in the course, when it was my turn I wasn't intimidated at all. As I started going through my slides and giving my talk, I noticed heads nodding in the audience. I thought, *Hey, I think I can do this!* It was the first time in my professional life I can remember having that thought.

Being moved over into John's program set another chain of events in motion.

These events would have equally far-reaching implications for my life. When Life of Georgia threw me a lifeline in early 1981 by pulling me out of underwriting and setting me up with John Drago, they also hired a young woman named Loveanne to replace me in my old job. Loveanne was smart as a whip, and I liked her a lot. Apparently she liked me, too. That spring we started dating.

Loveanne was the best thing that could have happened to me.

One Sunday, I brought her home to Salem to meet my parents and have lunch. I'd done this with several other girls I'd dated, but this Sunday the routine went a little differently. Halfway through lunch, my mom excused herself and went out to the pantry, quietly beckoning me to come join her. I went in and said, "Hey, Mom. What's up?"

She gave me a *now listen to me* look and said, "Johnny, you need to marry her."

As usual, I agreed with my mom. In the spring of 1982, a year after we met, Loveanne and I were married. It was one of the best decisions, probably *the* best, of my life.

Sometimes people experience dramatic events in their lives, turning points where something suddenly goes *Boom!* From that moment on, their lives change radically. I wonder, though, how often those moments really go *Boom!* Or do we see their importance only later on? For me, change has always seemed like more of an evolutionary than a revolutionary thing. In retrospect, I can see specific events and decisions that did in fact put me on a different path, like being placed in that program with John Drago. But they were seldom big, dramatic things that struck me as significant while they were actually happening.

Still, there have been a few times when things did seem to come to a head. These times are what you might call *defining moments*. One of those came right on the heels of getting married to Loveanne.

Coming out of college, I hadn't been super motivated or felt like I aspired to any great accomplishments. But things were different now. I became much more grounded and driven. It wasn't just that I was married; I was married to *Loveanne*.

Suddenly, I knew it was time to make a change. I was plugged into a whole new *why*.

For one thing, the commute just wasn't working anymore. After our wedding, Loveanne and I moved into a rental condo in Clarkston, a town right off the 285 loop not far from the apartment I shared with my buddies. Every morning we were riding into Atlanta together to go to work at Life of Georgia. This might sound romantic, but that's not exactly how it was working out.

I'm a wake-up-and-get-moving kind of guy, one of those people who is always saying, "Hurry up! Let's get going!" Loveanne, not so much. My wife is not a morning person. I expect you can see where I'm going with this. Loveanne and I pretty quickly figured out that if we kept driving in to work together, we would probably find ourselves in divorce court.

Of course, our commuting situation wasn't the real issue. Something bigger was going on for me. That bigger issue was something that's green and rhymes with *honey*. When I was living the single life, if I had enough cash for a good weekend coming up, I was good to go. Things were different now. We were married and starting to talk about raising a family.

One of my best friends from high school, J. Mark Davis, had also been a classmate at UGA, where he majored in accounting. Mark passed his CPA exam and got a job right out of college with Price Waterhouse over in Birmingham. (Mark continued to do well for himself. Today he is president of the Coca Cola Scholars Foundation and oversees millions of dollars every year in scholarships to high school seniors who exhibit strong leadership potential.)

Mark's success suddenly seemed terribly significant to me. It dawned on me that being the funniest one at the college party was no longer the principal metric of success. Now the scoreboard had to do with making a better income. Mark was pulling down more than $20,000 a year. My best friend had a *good* job. I had *a* job.

And it wasn't just that. Something larger had changed.

Growing up as an only child, I'd always been very content to be by myself. I got along with other people well, but at the same time, being on my own was a state that just came naturally to me. Now that changed. For the first time in my life, I had someone else to think about. I wasn't just *me* anymore. Now I was *us*.

By this time, I'd been working at Life of Georgia for close to two years, and I knew I didn't want to work there for the rest of my life. Just having a job wasn't going to cut it anymore. I needed a *career*. I still didn't know exactly what I was going to do next—but I knew it needed to besomething better than what I was doing.

I knew *why* I needed to do it.

Keep Moving Forward

At the same time that John Drago was watching us and training us, I was watching him. I'd been looking hard at what John was doing—not just at what he was teaching *us* to do, but at what *he* was doing. These management consultants traveled; they dealt with people in lots of different situations; they got paid well. That all sounded like something I'd like to do.

I didn't think my particular mix of skills (whatever they were) lined up with any of the existing jobs there at Life of Georgia. I started thinking that maybe I could do what John was doing. So one day I sat down with him and asked him, what did it take to be a management consultant?

"Well, John," he said, "you have to go get yourself an MBA."

I took the GMAT to see if I even had a shot at it. According to the test results, I should give it a go. I decided to go back to school and get my MBA.

This presented a logistical issue. If I was going to go to school every evening after work, ideally I needed to be working somewhere closer to home so I could get home from work in enough time to have dinner and then ride the MARTA rapid transit downtown to Georgia State University to go to class. I decided it was time to leave Life of Georgia and get a job closer to my apartment—correction: *our* apartment.

I didn't know what kind of job, exactly, or where it might lead. All I knew was that the river was branching—and this seemed like the right fork to take.

One Monday not long after this I was home from work sick, sitting in our little living room in Clarkston and looking through the want ads in the *Atlanta Journal-Constitution*, when I noticed one that read:

Rapidly growing insurance company looking for bright young college graduates.

Hey! I was young, and I was a college graduate. I wasn't completely sure about the "bright" part, but two out of three ain't bad. The position was described as "business analyst." Whatever that meant, chances were good John Drago's training had gotten me at least a little prepared for it. I'd already worked for an insurance firm for two years, so that had to count for something. The best part, though, was the thing that caught my eye in the first place: The company was located barely 10 minutes away from our apartment. I decided to apply.

The company was called A.L. Williams.

I went in, talked to their personnel department, and filled out an application. They offered me a job for $19,200 a year. That was a good $3,000 more than the $16,000 I was making at Life of Georgia. And here was the clincher: They had a deal where, if you were working on a master's in business administration and you kept your grades at a B or above, they would reimburse your tuition. For Loveanne and me, that was huge. All I had to do was make sure I kept my grades up.

The next day, I went into Life of Georgia and turned in my resignation.

As I said, life turns on the smallest of decisions, and you never know which ones will prove the most significant.

The shaping events in your life, those moments that in hindsight prove to be crucial turning points, are often events that just seem to happen, out of the blue, the chance confluence of unpredictable circumstances. But the truth is that they don't "just happen." Most times, they happen because you're taking action in the direction of your *why*. You may not be able to plan the results, but that's okay. If you keep moving forward, focusing on incremental improvement, you'll put yourself in their path.

This is one of the most deceptively simple leadership principles there is: *keep moving forward*. People won't follow you if you're sitting in the corner sucking your thumb and talking about how bad things are. They'll only follow you if you're going somewhere.

If you're sitting around waiting for something to happen, you're a stationary target for the bad things of life. A moving target is harder to hit. If you're in motion, then you're going some-where, even if you're not sure exactly where that is. And as long as you're in motion, you can always shift your course. It's an awful lot easier to steer a car that's moving than one that's sitting still.

> People won't follow you if you're sitting in the corner sucking your thumb and talking about how bad things are.

Waking up every day and aiming to be a little better than you were the day before is maybe what Campbell means by "answering a call." I don't know. I've just tried to pay attention to what's going on around me and make the right decision about which foot to put where.

Wrestle the Alligator in Front of You

There's a great saying in the military that applies just as well to life as it does to the battlefield: Every plan is great—until the first shot is fired. No one knew this better than Winston Churchill, who took office as prime minister of England in 1940 during a time of extreme crisis. Not only was the first shot already fired, but Europe had already been plunged into world war. Churchill's story is an epic tutorial in principled response to chaos and adversity.

"Plans are of little importance," Churchill once said, though he also added, "but planning is essential." (George Patton put it a little more bluntly: "A good plan, violently executed now, is better than a perfect plan next week.")

One of Churchill's great strengths—one among many—was his ability to hang tough and stay the course. Another was his fearlessness in taking immediate action when immediate action was warranted by the circumstances.

I've been to visit the Cabinet War Rooms, the underground complex where Churchill ran the war effort. His desk is still there, preserved in his office, and on it there sits a box he put there with a label that says, "Action This Day." Not an IN box. A TODAY box. Whether it was five in the afternoon or 2:30 in the morning, the prime minister was not leaving his desk until the last thing in that box got handled. I can't say I've always succeeded, but in my career I have sought every day to follow that example.

I may not be big on detailed long-term planning, but I'm very big on being in motion, in action, right now. I drive people crazy when they travel with me, because I never check a suitcase. I'll do a 10-day tour through Europe with nothing but a duffle bag. When we get off our plane, I'm not in the mood to wait around. For me, it's off the plane and go. When I go through that airport, I'm *moving*. Even if I'm not sure where I'm going, I'm going to get there fast.

A lot of people seem as if they're trying to avoid the present. Maybe they do this in the hope that if they just keep their eyes on a better future, then whatever's going on right now will sort itself out.

It won't. Whatever challenges or problems you're dealing with today, they are not going to get better with age. The only thing they're going to do with age is get worse. Here's my approach to problems: I don't want to talk about it. I don't want to think about it. I don't want to form a committee to study it for the next 18 months. Whatever the problem or challenge is, I want to get it dealt with *today*. I believe you've got to get up every day and wrestle the alligator that's in front of you. And then move on to the next one.

There is a difference between a dream and a pipe dream. The difference is that a pipe dream isn't real. What makes a dream real is that the person dreaming it knows how to take action and deal with immediate problems, instead of sitting around waiting for someone else to deal with the problems or hoping they'll change on their own.

Go get it done. Quit talking about what you're going to do. Quit writing down what you're going to do, and go do it. Get after it. Go make it happen now.

As soon as word got around that I'd turned in my resignation, I was called into the office of a senior vice president by the name of Gerald Padgett. Mr. Padgett ran the New Business division. In fact, he'd been my boss when I was still in underwriting. So here I was, being called onto the carpet by my former boss. He was a man more than twice my age who had a heck of a lot more experience than I did.

"John," he said, "you're a bright young man. But you're making a dumb mistake."

I wasn't sure how to respond to that. Maybe I could have pointed out that nobody at Life of Georgia was offering me an extra $3,000 a year to stay on, but that didn't seem like a smart thing to say. So I didn't say anything.

> Quit talking about what you're going to do. Quit writing down what you're going to do, and go do it.

"I honestly cannot believe you're doing this," Mr. Padgett continued. "They really like you here, in that training program you're doing. Stay with it and you'll end up in management. But that company you're leaving us to join? It's nothing but a fly-by-night operation. A few years down the road they won't even exist anymore. You're throwing your life away."

Was I throwing my life away? I didn't think so. In any case, this didn't feel like some major career decision because I didn't plan on being at that new job very long anyway. This was only temporary. I just needed a place to clock in and earn the rent while I went to school. Once I'd earned that MBA, I was going to go become a management consultant and join a big consulting firm. I was headed for a whole other career, right?

Besides, it *was* a lot closer to our apartment.

Mr. Padgett told me this place was a fly-by-night operation that wouldn't last much past the expiration date on my car's inspection sticker. Maybe he was right. Maybe it was a fly-by-night operation, and maybe it wouldn't last long. But that didn't bother me much. All I needed was for A.L. Williams to stick around long enough for me to get my degree, and then I'd be out of there.

Of course, things didn't exactly turn out that way.

PRACTICE #1

Decide Who You Are

Having goals and big dreams is important, but there's something even more important. It is something that comes first: deciding what kind of person you are. Even before you know exactly what you want to *do*, you can decide who you want to *be*, and live your life accordingly.

- Decide what you believe and who you are in the process of becoming. You can't change your background or your past. Ultimately, what kind of person you turn out to be is your decision.

- Look for the best in people and do what you can to bring that out in them. Look for the good in yourself, too. Focus on bringing those qualities out in yourself.

- Keep moving forward. Wake up every day and aim to be better than yesterday. Be willing to improve a little at a time. Incremental improvement takes patience, persistence, and faith. The payoff is more than worth it.

- Whatever issue is facing you, deal with it today. Don't wait. The only thing problems do with age is get worse. Let the future take care of itself. Focus on wrestling the alligator that's in front of you. Life turns on the smallest of decisions, and you never know which will prove the most significant.

ACTION STEP

List the top two or three people whom you most admire, along with what it is about them specifically that you seek to emulate in your own life.

CHAPTER 2

The People Business

Shine Your Light on Others

There is no limit to the amount of good you can do
if you don't care who gets the credit.

—RONALD REAGAN

O n a Monday morning in the fall of 1982, I nosed my car onto
I-285, drove two exits north, and got off at Tucker, a community on the northeast outskirts of Atlanta. About 10 minutes
after I'd stepped out the front door of our little Clarkston condo,
I was pulling into an office complex parking lot for my first day
at A.L. Williams. *Ahh*, I thought, now *that's* a commute.

I slid into an empty slot, parked, and looked around. I noticed
a big old Winnebago there. On the side, like a billboard splayed
onto the flanks of a commercial long-haul 18-wheeler, was the
A.L. Williams name and logo. Below was a line of 10-mile-high
type that read, "Mobile Recruiting and Training Vehicle."

"Well, this is . . . different," I said to myself. "I don't know
exactly what it is, but it's definitely different."

That right there turned out to be the understatement of my
career. A.L. Williams was different, all right. It was different

in so many ways that it took me years to grasp just what this animal was.

A.L. Williams was different in how it structured its sales force and in the kind of people who made up that force. It was different in how everyone involved saw what it was they were doing there and how they all held a fervent devotion to a common mission. Most of all, it was different in how the company viewed and treated its people. Its approach was a direct expression of the philosophy of its founder.

Though I didn't know it when I started there, the founder's philosophy would remind me an awful lot of how my parents viewed the world and would reinforce the values I'd learned while growing up in Salem. These values held that leadership is all about shining your light on other people, rather than promoting yourself.

A Business Is a Community

When I was growing up in Salem, there was a general store in the center of town, called H.L. "Roy" Moore's General Merchandise. Roy and Helen Moore's general store wasn't just a business. It was a social institution. It was the place where everyone congregated. In addition to its shelves and barrels of goods, it had a sitting area where people would sit themselves down, rest, and talk. It seemed like we went there almost every evening. In many ways, it was the center of the community.

Helen Moore, who was one of my mom's best friends, was also in Stanley Home Products, one of those great old household-name direct sales companies, like Avon, Tupperware, or Fuller Brush. The way Miss Helen sold Stanley was, she would take orders from everyone in the community, and then, once a quarter or so, she would hold a bingo night at the community center.

Everyone would come play bingo. If you won, you'd win Stanley prizes. She'd have her catalogues there, and everyone would mill around after the game and order the stuff they needed.

Growing up, all I ever saw my mom clean with was Stanley Degreaser. Every hairbrush we owned was from Stanley. We had more Stanley products than a dog has fleas. Our home was like a Stanley showroom. Helen was a high-energy lady, the kind of person other people seemed to revolve around. I didn't have the words for it as a kid, but I do now. Helen Moore was a natural-born salesperson.

It never occurred to me that you could sell insurance this way, with ordinary folks like Helen selling to their friends and community. But that's what they were doing, more or less, at my new employer's company. Rather than having a full-time "professional" sales force, A.L. Williams sold its products through a network of independent agents whose earnings were pure 1099 commissions, not W-2 wages. In other words, they weren't on the payroll. These were not salespeople by profession. By and large, they were firefighters, policemen, school teachers, and UPS drivers. They were folks who had the most regular of regular jobs and were moonlighting with their A.L. Williams businesses to earn some supplemental household income.

At the same time, A.L. Williams was very different from a business like Stanley Home Products in some significant ways. It had to be. At A.L. Williams, people were not selling cleaning supplies but life insurance and mutual funds, which are highly regulated commodities. Before someone could go out and start selling the products they had to go through a certification process and become licensed to sell insurance or mutual funds or both.

There was also a whole other layer to the business, beyond the actual selling. A.L. Williams's reps were also empowered to recruit other reps into their organization and earn overrides on *their* sales, and on the sales of those *they* recruited, and so on. In other words, there was a very real financial opportunity here not only to earn income directly by selling insurance, but also to build an income-generating organization of other agents doing the same thing.

This was more than a structural tweak. This was central to the company's philosophy. It meant that, for these thousands and thousands of independent reps, a big part of the business was about recruiting, training, supporting, and leading their groups of other reps, in addition to selling insurance policies.

Hence, the need for the "Mobile Recruiting and Training Vehicle."

It meant that as an A.L. Williams rep, you weren't just there to help build the company. You were building, to use a phrase I would hear probably thousands of times during the eighties "your own company within a company."

Throughout my childhood, Roy and Helen Moore's general store had been more than a store. It had been the hub of our little community and way of life. As it turned out, the company I'd now gone to work for was more than an insurance business. It was the hub of a far-flung community of thousands of like-minded people who were there to support and build up each other as well as their own businesses.

Of course, when I took the job at A.L. Williams I didn't know about any of this. I didn't have the faintest idea that the company's business had anything to do with recruiting teams or developing leadership in people, or about giving people the opportunity to build their own "company within a company." All I really knew about the company was that it was based on an idea summed up in the slogan, "Buy Term and Invest the Difference."

I didn't know what that phrase meant, but I would soon learn. I would also learn that, in the insurance world, that slogan had started a war.

A Company on a Mission

A.L. Williams wasn't just a company, it was a *cause*. Its people were on a mission to transform the life insurance industry.

Art Williams, the A.L. Williams founder, was not a business school grad or career financial guy. He was a Georgia high school football coach who had gotten incensed one day when he realized that everyday Americans were getting ripped off by big insurance companies. Instead of just complaining, Art did something about it. He decided to build his own company. But he didn't just want to build his own little agency. He wanted to take on the entire industry and transform it.

"Buy term and invest the difference," also known in the business as *BTID*, was a better approach than traditional whole life insurance. A whole life policy has a savings component as well as death protection. The problem is that whole life insurance has a very low rate of return. In the event of your death, your loved ones only get the face value of the policy rather than your policy amount and your savings component. With BTID, you get pure protection on your life as well as the ability to build up your own savings. In the event of your death, your loved ones get both your policy amount *and* your savings. Art wasn't interested in selling expensive policies with big margins to people who could afford it. He wanted to sell more sensible policies to people who *needed* it. People on a budget. People on a shoestring. Middle-income people. Ordinary people.

In fact, the goal wasn't ultimately to simply sell people these products. The real goal was to give them a financial education, to help them learn how to avoid the common pitfalls middle-income families typically faced: too much debt, not enough savings, and either no insurance or insurance that was way more expensive than it needed to be.

This strategy was raising the competition's hackles. In the traditional life insurance industry, nobody *replaced* anyone's insurance. If you had it, you had it. And here was this maverick guy who was not only replacing people's insurance but saying that those other guys' products were rip-offs. Not surprisingly, this approach was not popular with the big boys of the business. Art and his little outfit were going up against some of the most powerful companies in the United States, and it ticked them off big time.

What's more, Art was not shy about what he wanted to do. Art didn't view these other guys as friendly competitors. He viewed them as the enemy, pure and simple. Art put it this way: When you coach football, if you're playing a team you respect, with a coach you respect and players you respect, and you're up by a couple of touchdowns late in the game, you come to the line slow, take your time, let the clock run. You know you're going to win, there's no point rubbing it in. At the end of the game you take a knee and show your respect to your opponent. That's what you do with a coach you respect.

It's different if you're playing a coach you don't like and a team that's corrupt and doing bad things. In that case, you may have a three-touchdown lead, but you hustle up to the line with every new down; you run those plays fast and hard. You don't just want to win; you want to crush them. That's exactly how Art saw his company's role within its industry. He didn't just want to win. He wanted to run up the score and stomp them.

All of which did not exactly win Art a lot of friends in the industry. If you listened to his critics talk about him, you would have thought he was a beast from the pit of hell.

To Art, attacks like that were just more fuel. Some people get intimidated by criticism. Not Art. You throw a rock at him; he'll shoot a bazooka back.

This was all totally foreign to me. I was brought up to be a peacemaker. I don't care for confrontation and don't like it when people attack me. They say, "Sticks and stones will break my bones, but words will never hurt me." Everyone knows that plain isn't true. Words can hurt, all right. Words can hurt you way more than sticks and stones. What words do is worse than breaking your bones. They get under your skin and start affecting how you feel about yourself. I like to be liked. I was raised to always be the first to apologize. That was ingrained in me as a child, and that's always been a part of my business style.

Not Art. The more people attacked him, calling him a crook, a con man, and all kinds of ugly things, the more it energized him. I honestly don't think I could have gone through what he went through and just kept going. No, I take that back. I *know for sure* I couldn't have. Art is probably the most mentally tough person I've ever encountered.

Art's toughness was a mighty good thing for us because these companies tried to destroy A.L. Williams every way they could. They attacked the upstart company for being a fly-by-night operation, an illegal scam, an unscrupulous con game. They howled that A.L. Williams was a Pied Piper act, pulling thousands of customers away from their good old traditional whole-life policies and replacing them with sub-par term insurance. And this upstart company, they said, was so poorly financed it probably wouldn't even be around to pay on its claims! There were PR campaigns, lobbying efforts, smear tactics, and legal battles. It was all-out war.

No wonder Gerald Padgett had told me I was throwing my career away.

By the time I joined A.L. Williams, they were five years into the fight with the big dogs of the insurance industry, and the underdog was winning. A.L. Williams was growing like a thousand acres of weeds, which was exactly why they were hiring people like me.

In March 1980, A.L. Williams opened their office in Tucker where I would soon be working. They processed twenty-five hundred new applications in their first month. By March 1982, just two years later, they were processing new applications at nearly ten times that rate. In June 1983, A.L. Williams had more than $2 billion worth of life insurance in force. By that fall it was close to $4 billion.

The crazy growth surged on through the year and overflowed into 1984. By July 1984, A.L. Williams had already matched our total production for the entire previous year. That November, we did some $6 billion in new business. One month later, with a sales force of 80,000 licensed reps, A.L. Williams blew past Prudential to become the number one producer of life insurance in the United States.

So much for "fly by night."

Make People Feel Important (Because They *Are*)

When I started at A.L. Williams, my job title was "business analyst." What that meant in practical terms was that I was a troubleshooter. And there was plenty of trouble to shoot. All that crazy, rapid growth was creating a logistical nightmare between us and our underwriter.

In the insurance world, the *agency* sells and writes insurance policies for customers. The *underwriter* supplies the financial underpinning as well as actuarial muscle that does the serious number crunching and analytical heavy lifting—the kind of work I'd been slogging through at that little desk for my first year at Life of Georgia. You can think of agency and underwriter as something like seller and manufacturer. A.L. Williams was an insurance agency. Their policies were underwritten by the Massachusetts Indemnity and Life Insurance Corporation (MILICO), which was owned by a California firm called Penn-Corp Financial.

While we (the agency) were based in Georgia, all PennCorp's computer systems and IT resources were out in California. This meant that the physical collecting, collating, and entering of applications and claims was happening there in Tucker, but all the data processing was happening on the other side of the country in Santa Monica. This was the early eighties. It was the era of big, although not always that fast or reliable, mainframes. Coordinating the field work for a sprawling and rapidly growing network of part-timers together with the complexities of central organizing and processing on the other side of the country was massively complicated.

My job, and the job of all the others like me, was to work in the spaces between the managers of the various departments and IT people in Santa Monica to fix problems. There was no telling what we'd be working on at any given time. Whatever was messed up, that's where we went.

During those early months as troubleshooter at large, I learned a great deal about the logistics and mechanics of the company. I still didn't really grasp the nature of what this thing was all about. That began to change in early 1983 when I attended a regional meeting in one of the hotel ballrooms in downtown Atlanta. I'd been with the company for about six months, and this was my first big event. There were maybe 2,000 people in attendance. It was also the first time I ever heard Art speak to a crowd. I knew he was good. But no way was I prepared for what I witnessed that night.

At UGA I'd heard plenty of professors address classes that filled auditoriums. In the more than three decades since that time, I've heard hundreds of speakers give talks, including some of the most renowned business icons, political leaders, and famous professional speakers in the world. Art tops them all. To this day, I've never heard anything like it.

> A good speaker talks *at* you. A great communicator speaks *to* you.

It wasn't that Art was an especially polished presenter. In fact, that wasn't it at all. You could tell that was a football coach up there on that stage. It didn't feel like a business presentation or CEO's speech as much as a rousing half-time locker-room talk only on a massive scale.

Wow, I thought. *This guy's a powerful speaker.* He was more than a powerful speaker. He was a great *communicator*.

There's a difference between being a good speaker and a good communicator. A good speaker is exactly that: someone who can speak well. There are plenty of people out there who can perform a speech with skill. A great communicator, that's something else entirely. A great communicator can stand up in front of a group of people and sense what's going on in their hearts and heads and know how to minister to where they are and what they need to hear. There are plenty of people who can stand up and give a great speech and yet are completely disconnected from their audience. Their speech has nothing to do with how people feel. A good speaker talks *at* you. A great communicator speaks *to* you.

That's what Art was doing. He was speaking to *you*. He didn't just inspire people. Any charismatic presenter with even a little bit of training and experience can do that. He *connected* with them. For every one of us in that auditorium, he also painted a vivid picture of what it was we were all doing together and why it mattered.

Here was the company's mission, as I began to understand it:

Death happens. Households struggle. Life is hard, and anyone who tells you different is a liar. What A.L. Williams was about was helping families take a few simple steps that would help them weather the bad times and more fully enjoy the good times. The mission was to make sure families were properly protected, that they could have a meaningful plan to get out of debt, and that they had a simple, practical path to accumulate funds so they could retire with dignity.

This was a company that did good things for ordinary families.

Moreover, Art wasn't talking just about insurance or the financial prospects of the company and its agents. As Art spoke to the crowd, he was talking to them about their lives, their goals, and their dreams. It began to dawn on me that this company was about something more than building business. In a fundamental way, it was about *building people.* For all Art's colorful personality and zeal for his mission, it was clear that the man wasn't up there on stage showboating. In fact, he didn't really talk about himself at all. The main thing Art talked to the crowd about was them: how great they were, how great their future was, how honorable a thing it was that they were doing.

Not him. *Them.*

There's a story about a journalist in England in the late 1800s who went to dine with both William Gladstone and his rival, Benjamin Disraeli, to see which one she judged the better man.

"After talking with Mr. Gladstone," she reported, "I came away feeling he was the smartest man in England. But then I dined with Mr. Disraeli and quickly forgot about Mr. Gladstone. Because after talking with Mr. Disraeli, I felt as though I was the smartest woman in England."

That was exactly what Art Williams was doing in that auditorium. He didn't impress that crowd with how important *he* was. He made everyone in that room feel important themselves.

It Doesn't Take Much to Shine Your Light on Others

Watching Art up there on stage that evening reminded me of something we'd been studying in graduate school, a principle known as the Hawthorne Effect.

In the early 1900s, the Hawthorne Works in Chicago commissioned a study to see if they could make their workers more productive. They divided the workers into two groups. Then they told one group they were going to be participating in a study on productivity. All they actually did for this group was to make the lights in the factory a tiny bit brighter. Yet productivity soared.

The researchers concluded that the higher productivity was caused not by the brighter light but by the fact that the people suddenly felt special because someone was studying them. But as far as I was concerned, whichever factor you thought was the key—better light bulbs or more attention—they came down to the same thing. They were both about shining more light on people.

The fascinating thing was that the change itself was very slight. It wasn't as if the researchers told those workers how great they were or lavished all kinds of praise on them. They just told them they were going to study them. It doesn't sound like a big deal, but the point was that suddenly someone was *paying attention* to them. That was maybe the biggest message I took away from that study. It doesn't take much to make a difference.

The month I turned seven, the Civil Rights Act of 1964 was passed into law. For the next few years schools began integrating according to what they called "freedom of choice." This meant that if you were a white kid and wanted to go to the African-American school, you could. If you were an African-American kid and wanted to go to the white school, you could do that too. At least that was the theory. In practice, what it meant was that the schools mostly stayed segregated.

Integration was a very highly charged issue in our little community. There was never any violence or rioting, but there were marches and demonstrations and an awful lot of talk. Often, that talk got pretty heated. None of it made much sense to me.

The first time any African-American students attended Ficquett Elementary School in Covington was in the fall of 1966, when I was entering fourth grade. Our grade had four classes of about thirty kids each. Since there were maybe four or five black kids in total who joined my school that year, there was about one new student per class.

I remember my mom driving me to school that first day. These days it's no more than a five-minute drive to downtown Covington from where I grew up. Back then, we lived on a dirt road, and it took a little while to get to town. When we got to school, we saw people from the local media clustered around, reporting on the big event and the town's reactions.

We pulled up in front of the school and Mom stopped the car, turned in her seat, and looked at me. "Johnny," she said.

"Now you remember—you were raised right, and you're a good boy. These kids who are coming to your school are scared. You understand? The first one you see, you walk up to them and welcome them to your school. You make them feel at home."

I nodded and told her I would do that. Then I got out of the car and headed into school. The first African-American boy I saw sitting there in the classroom, I went up to him and said, "Hi, I'm Johnny Addison. I just wanna welcome you to our school."

The boy's name was Horace Johnson. Horace and I became good friends. We're still good friends today. He grew up to study law and eventually became the first African-American judge elected to serve in Newton County, Georgia. My younger son Tyler clerked for Horace one summer when he was getting ready to go to law school.

Horace says he remembers walking out of school between a row of state patrol officers who flanked him and the few other African-American students in order to block their view of the protests happening on the street outside the school. To this day, I'm in awe of the courage it took those young boys and girls to do what they did.

> A little recognition goes a long way, but you have to keep it going.

I also remember thinking, *So what is all the fuss about?* So these kids were a different color and from a different background than us. So what? I mean, how hard was it to walk up to Horace and introduce myself? After 12 words, we had a friendship that has enriched both our lives for decades.

It really doesn't take much to shine your light on others. And you'll find a whole lot of light comes shining back.

By the way, there was one more thing about the Hawthorne Effect study that caught my attention. The moment the study was over, the Hawthorne workers' productivity sank back to its previous level. There was a message there too. When you shine your light on others it *is* a big deal. A little recognition goes a long way, but you have to keep it going.

You can't grow plants by giving them light once or twice a month. It turns out the same thing goes for people. It's important to give people your attention, but it's equally important to *keep* doing it, and not just every once in a while.

Leaders Work for Their People

In 1984, I got a promotion. I was moved from my position as troubleshooter where I was responsible for field compensation and licensing. Now I was in charge of making sure that commission checks were accurate and went out on time; that the apparatus for getting people licensed in all the different states was running smoothly; and that we were keeping up with the constant and complex progression of regulatory change.

Throughout my first two years at A.L. Williams, I'd been fairly well removed from much of the action on the front lines, working totally on projects at the home office. I'd had absolutely no contact with the field and really hadn't grasped the nature of the organization. Given the kind of work I did, I might have been at any other large insurance firm.

Now that changed. For the first time, I started having regular contact with the field. Before I knew it, I was on the phone with the senior leaders every day, helping solve the problems they faced. Most of this work was one-on-one, and I built a lot of relationships that I still have today.

Licensing was massively complicated and getting more complicated all the time. In their effort to squash the upstart A.L. Williams, the big insurance companies were constantly influencing regulators to make licensing requirements more and more difficult. With 50 states came 50 different sets of regulations and standards and processes, which made for a never-ending battle with escalating complexity.

Compensation wasn't all that simple either. Again, this was the eighties, and a great deal more was done by hand and on paper than it is today. When I'd been a troubleshooter, I'd dealt with the challenges of getting accurate and timely information from Tucker to Santa Monica and back. Now I was dealing with getting accurate and timely information from little field offices scattered all over the country to Tucker and back. A lot of the senior guys in the sales force still think of me today as the kid they used to call when there were problems with the checks.

Beyond the technical challenges, my new responsibilities started giving me new insights into who these field leaders were. As I got to know these people and work through their problems with them, I began to understand just how much they were driven by a mission to foster success for the other reps in their organizations. I saw how much they did for these folks, and how hard they worked to get it right. I began to realize that "leader" wasn't just a field title. These guys and gals felt an enormous responsibility to the people in their groups. They were working their butts off to make sure the business was working for them.

When I was a young boy, I would go with my dad now and then to the textile plant in Atlanta where he worked. Everyone there called him Mr. Addison. I could see how much they all respected him. It made a big impression on me. Even though I didn't understand anything about how a company really operated, I could tell that they saw my father as the guy who more or less kept it all going. It made me proud of him.

One year, he was promoted to a position that gave him responsibility over an entire area of the plant. He moved into a glassed-in supervisor's office, right out on the manufacturing floor, where he could see everyone and they could see him. Later he got an even bigger promotion, to executive vice president. Now he was one of the top five people in command. At this point, he was supposed to move to the executive building. It was separate from the plant and had secretaries, nice offices, and various amenities that were exclusive to the executives.

But my father wouldn't do it. He insisted on keeping his old office out on the floor. There he could be in the middle of things and with the folks who were doing the work.

At the time, I probably couldn't have told you just what it was I learned. I knew I'd learned something important from my dad's choice, something that would stay with me always. It was only many years later that I began to grasp what it was.

The way my father saw it, those people weren't working for *him*.

He was working for *them*.

Back in 1977, when he created A.L. Williams, Art said his goal was to build a company where the sales force was king. The first time I heard that I thought about my dad, in his glass office right out there in the middle of the shop room floor at Fulton Bag Cotton Mill, refusing to "graduate" to an office in the executive building removed from where the workers were.

No wonder I clicked with this company's culture.

That sales-force-first concept meant building a company with no limits on recruiting, no limits on promotion, no protected territories, and no unfair limits on growth. A sales force that offered unlimited positions at the top. In other words, it was basically upside down from the typical corporate concept. This army of salespeople wasn't working for the company. The company was working for *them*.

Art's concept was so radical that when he first went looking for an underwriter, the top executives of nearly a dozen big insurance companies told him he was dreaming and turned him down flat. Of course, he *was* dreaming. And over the years, thousands and thousands of people all signed on to the same dream.

My Post-Graduate Course in Leadership

For my first few years at A.L. Williams, I was taking all this in from a bit of a distance. Once I started working on marketing projects with Art himself, I got the opportunity to observe it all at close hand.

They say your history gets richer as you age. Sometimes these days when I'm being introduced before speaking at an event, I'll hear the host describe me as "Art Williams's advisor in those early years. . . ." It's a very nice thing to say, but it isn't true. I was not an *advisor* of Art's by any stretch of reality. In reality, I was a slightly glorified "gofer." And it had nothing whatsoever to do with my job description.

This new role started happening in 1985, the same year we graduated from that little office park in Tucker to a new and much larger home office complex in Duluth, Georgia. That was the year I started playing a role in the company's marketing department.

Actually, Art didn't so much "have" a marketing department. It was more like Art *was* marketing. He had a full-blown publications and communications apparatus at his command with a team of writers, designers, artists, and others. If Art got mad about something someone said about us, he could have a brochure countering it in the mail the next day. It was always Art who drove the message.

As the company continued wrestling with the constant barrage of attacks from the insurance industry, Art was constantly putting together print pieces that went after the industry, exposed the corruption, and educated consumers. Pieces with titles like "The Magic of Compound Interest" or "Why A.L. Williams Is Right for the American Consumer" featured illustrations that compared our term policies to traditional whole life policies. My boss at the time was a man named Rick Mathis, who was in charge of Agency Administration. Rick was also one of the guys Art would bring into meetings he held to brainstorm these marketing ideas. One day in 1985, Rick dragged me along.

I really had no business being there. I was not remotely qualified to be in Art's inner circle. I was quite a few rungs on the ladder below the people who fit that description. I think my only qualification for being in the room was that as an MBA student, I had a Texas Instruments business analyst's calculator. Up to this point, I'd had next to no contact with our CEO. I would see him coming in and out of the building every now and then. But most of the time, he was on the road motivating the sales force and building the business. When he was at the home office, I had no occasion to interact with him. But for whatever reason, there I was.

At one point I said, "Hey, I've got an idea." I went on to outline a thought about a presentation he might do. He liked it, and they went with it. Soon I was regularly being pulled into Art's office. Art would say, "John, here's what I'm doing. Go get me this." I would go collect rows of numbers and data for him to use in his next piece.

The following year, Art launched a network of satellite dishes placed in our offices around the country. We were the first company to use satellite television this way. He called it ALW-TV and started doing weekly Monday-morning broadcasts, which consisted of Art motivating, inspiring, and launching whatever new things we had to launch.

I was still in grad school at the time. Georgia State had a large insurance department in its business school. I went to the school library one evening and started combing through all the industry periodicals, seeing what kinds of articles I could find that might have interesting facts and figures or other tidbits in there. Especially, I looked for things Art could use to attack the competition.

One day I'd brought a folder of this stuff to a meeting. "Hey, Art," I said. "I was down at Georgia State the other night and got a bunch of stuff you might be interested in."

He took the folder and started going through it. He looked up at me and said, "Hey, this is good stuff." He paged through it for another minute, then looked up at me again and said, "Look, John, here's what I want you to do. Every Monday morning, come to my office and bring me good crap."

So, ladies and gentlemen, that's the truth of my "advisor" role with Art Williams in those early years. That was my assignment: to bring Art good crap.

Soon Art started calling me his "numbers guy." The irony was not lost on me. I'm not a complete ignoramus when it comes to numbers. I can find my way around a balance sheet when necessary. But "the guy with the amazingly mathematical mind" would not be a description that would lead anyone who knows me to say, "Oh right, you mean Addison." The situation did not exactly have me playing to my strengths.

That didn't matter. What I was actually doing for Art wasn't really the point. Being around him, working with him and his whole creative team, *that* was the point. It had an incredibly important influence on the course of my career. It gave me the chance to study how he communicated, how he motivated people, how he created energy in those around him. When Art gave me a task to do, or for that matter whenever I observed him give anyone else a task, I would watch, listen, and think, "Now why is he doing that? For what purpose? What's he really doing here?"

Watching Art, I began to understand how much of what he did was driven by the singular goal of supporting the people in the field and giving them what they needed to do their jobs. When he would draw up a new comparison chart, or come up with a catchy new slogan or headline, it was always exactly what the sales force needed. He not only had his thumb on the pulse of the people who were doing the work and knew exactly what they were going through, he also *cared* about what they were going through.

> Real leadership is about building other people and shining your light on them, not on yourself.

The years from 1985 through 1989 were like an intensive postgraduate program in genuine leadership for me. And there was never a better professor than Art Williams.

Build Business by Building People

The biggest thing I learned from Art during those years was also probably the single most important lesson I learned during my entire career. Real leadership is about building other people and shining your light on them, not on yourself. It is the kind of leadership that not only works but also has a lasting impact.

Art wrote a number of books. In my view, the best of them was his 1985 book *Pushing Up People*. Even without reading the book, you get the core of Art's philosophy right there from the title. The way Art saw it, the purpose of business wasn't to go after sales. The purpose of business was to build people. Do that effectively and sales would follow as a natural result.

This philosophy meshed well with the values I'd grown up with. The idea that success in life comes from looking out for other people was ingrained in me from my earliest years. Now it became more explicit. I learned from Art that it was our job to make the field look good—not their job to make us look good.

Too many people in positions of leadership buy into their own press and start thinking they're a big deal. But being a leader is not the same thing as being a boss. The people around you are not there to make you a big deal—you're there to make them a big deal.

If you want to move other people, you have to put your own ego to the side.

Whenever you hear a leader giving a speech about how good things are, or about something great that's happened, count the number of times he or she uses the word *I*. *I promised this, I did that, I pledge that in the future . . . I, I, I.* So many people in leadership positions use *I* when things are good, and switch to *they* when things are bad. Politicians are also guilty of this, but leaders do it everywhere and in every industry. Business is no exception.

Real leaders who understand they are there to serve the team and not the other way around tend to use the word *we* when things are good. They understand instinctively how important it is to keep shining the light on others. If it isn't instinctive, then it's something they have taught themselves. When things are a success, they talk about how *we* did this, *we* accomplished that, *we're* going to do this in the future.

There is a time for *I*. It is when things are *not* going so well. When something's gone wrong or things aren't working, that's the time to use the word *I*. Even if the screw-up isn't your fault, even if you had absolutely nothing to do with it, even if you saw it coming and tried to warn against it, take responsibility. Step up. Own the problem. Be the one who lays out the solution or the pathway to finding a solution.

When things are bad, own the responsibility. When things go well, share the credit.

Here's the irony of it. When you do a good job of making everybody else around you feel good and look good, it's ultimately going to make you look good too. If you focus on shining your light on others, one of these days that light is going to turn around and shine right back on you.

I believe if more leaders in our country took that approach, we would be seeing a lot more success stories.

Throughout the early years, as I was absorbing all this on-the-job learning about business and leadership, I was also taking that MARTA high-speed rail every evening to downtown Atlanta to school to keep working on my actual graduate degree. The deal when I signed on with A.L. Williams back in 1982 had been simple: As long as I kept my grades at a B or above, the company would pay my tuition. I was determined to live up to my end of the bargain. Taking one class per quarter, I made it all the way through my required course work with only one B and the rest were all As.

> When things are bad, own the responsibility. When things go well, share the credit.

In the spring of 1988 our second son, Tyler, was born. (Kyle, our first, had come along in 1985.) A month later, I finished the final course for my degree. I was now the proud recipient of a master's in business administration from Georgia State University, finishing with a 3.95 grade point average. According to the path I'd scoped out for myself when I left my old job at Life of Georgia, now it was time to nail down a position as a management consultant with a big firm.

Except that in the meantime, a few things had changed.

Loveanne and I now had two kids and a nice little house in the quiet bedroom community of Snellville. My salary at A.L. Williams had well more than doubled, going from its original $19,200 to about $50,000. That was pretty good money, not the easiest thing to walk away from. More than that, I liked the company and liked the people. I liked what they were up to in the world. And I liked being a part of it.

So there it was. My big plan to set up shop as a management consultant was just that, a big plan. There's this wonderful saying, "Man plans, and God laughs." When I came up with that consulting career plan, God must have been having a good belly laugh. In any case, life happened, and as soon as the first shot was fired, that plan went out the window.

As it turned out, life had bigger plans for me than I had for myself.

Shine Your Light on Others

Real leadership, the kind of leadership that not only works but also has a lasting impact, is about building other people and shining your light on them, not on yourself. Real leaders understand they are here to work for the team, and not the other way around.

- A mediocre leader tries to impress people with how important he or she is. A great leader impresses upon people how important *they* are.

- People will be willing to do more and accomplish more when they feel recognized. A little recognition goes a long way, but you have to keep it going. You can't grow plants by giving them light once or twice a month. The same thing goes for people.

- When things are bad, own the responsibility. When things go well, share the credit.

- When you do a good job of making everybody else around you feel good and look good, it's ultimately going to make you look good too. If you focus on shining your light on others, one of these days that light is going to turn around and shine right back on you.

ACTION STEP

Make a list of three to five simple things you can do in your present business or career to build other people and shine your light on them. Every day, pick at least one action from this list to put into practice.

CHAPTER 3

Culture Shock

Build on Your Strengths

> Over the years, I've learned that a confident person doesn't concentrate or focus on their weaknesses—they maximize their strengths.
>
> —JOYCE MEYER

One blazingly hot day in the summer of 1990, Loveanne and I took the boys to the University of Georgia for Picture Day. It's an event held a few weeks before football season where you can bring your kids out onto the field and have their picture taken with the team mascot. As two-year-old Tyler and five-year-old Kyle stood there watching the proceedings and waiting their turn, I checked my watch for the umpteenth time. They were having a blast. I was nervous.

My problem didn't have anything to do with Picture Day. It had to do with the fact that our company was going through an upheaval.

Actually, calling it an "upheaval" is to put it in the mildest terms. "Seismic event" might be more like it. Thirteen years after the founding of A.L. Williams, the unthinkable had happened. Art was no longer in charge of the company. The next few years would be a trial for our company, a time when its ability to exist without its founder would be sorely tested. I didn't know it yet, but these years would also serve as a crucible for me, forging my career into something with a clear and distinct shape to it.

One thing that makes real leaders great is that they are keenly aware of their own strengths and weaknesses. Everyone has a vein of genius running on the inside, but real leaders learn how to tap into it and allow it rise to the surface. They seem to have a sense of their own path. They understand what they were put here to do.

Me, I didn't really have a clue. At this point in my career, although I'd been moving up through the ranks and had learned a tremendous amount, I really hadn't learned the most important part yet. I'd found a great job. But I hadn't yet found my *calling*.

Of course, I wasn't thinking about that as I checked my watch on Picture Day. I was focused on the more existential question of my family's financial future. After Kyle was born, Loveanne decided to stay home to be a full-time mom. Earlier in 1990 she had started going to class at night and on weekends to get a master's in social work. In the meantime, my career had taken off like a rocket, with salary increases to match. Our family depended on that salary. Now we had a full-blown household that depended on my income, which was suddenly in jeopardy.

Because while we were standing there having pictures taken with Uga the Bulldog, the company's new owners and the top executives were having a meeting in Duluth to decide who would stay and who would go. Smart money said as many as one-third of the home office employees would be out by day's end.

I didn't know whether I still had a job.

Businesses Aren't Just Organizations; They're Organisms

Partway through the event, I excused myself to go hunt down a payphone and call my boss, Rick Mathis.

"So, Rick," I said when I got him. "What's going on?"

"You're going to be in charge of licensing," he said. "And, yeah, you've got a job."

So *that* was a relief. Still, a lot of good people were gone. Those who were left were a bit shell-shocked. When Art walked out the doors for the last time, you could have split the Duluth headquarters into kindling with a lightning bolt and I don't think it would have stunned the people there any more than they already were. The reverberations of that day would echo throughout our company for years.

It was a long and complicated series of events and acquisitions that led to this turning point. In the early eighties our underwriter, PennCorp, was bought by a large company named American Can, which later changed its name to Primerica Corporation and was in turn eventually acquired by an incredibly talented and ambitious New York City entrepreneur named Sandy Weill. Our agency now had a shining new underwriter behind it, run by a brilliant Wall Street businessman. But the tide of change hadn't finished rolling in yet.

To Sandy, who was used to the chrome-and-glass skyscraper world of Manhattan high finance, our home-grown Georgia operation at A.L. Williams was a whole new experience. He fell in love with it. He loved the excitement of the sales force and the mission of helping middle-income families with their finances. He recognized both the company's uniqueness and its tremendous potential.

A year later, Sandy bought the A.L. Williams agency too.

At first, the plan was that both Art and Sandy would be there. Art would be the elder statesman, leading the charge for the field. But I knew in my gut that no matter how big this company got, it would never be big enough for these two out-sized personalities. The reality was that the company had a new owner. It didn't take long for that reality to become clear. In the summer of 1990, a year after selling the agency to Sandy, Art Williams left the company.

It's hard to convey just how total the change felt to those of us who were still standing after that summer's purge of corporate staff. Overnight our company went through as dramatic a transformation in culture as anyone could have possibly imagined.

Art ran his company like a football coach. He never wore a tie if he didn't absolutely have to. He did business in a golf shirt. And it wasn't just Art. Long before the days when "business casual" became cool, we *all* wore golf shirts with A.L. Williams' logos on them to work. At A.L. Williams, it was no unintended metaphor when we referred to the sales force as the people "out in the field." That was Art's ball team out there, and we were playing for a championship.

When this group of suits from New York showed up, it was like our office had all of a sudden been invaded by a species from another planet. You couldn't have come up with two more radically different views of business if you'd tried. Art's view: you build a company the same way you build a football team. It's all about helping them win out on the field. In the guys from New York's view, you build a business like a business. It's about the shareholders' bottom line.

Our new CEO, Don Cooper, was a good guy and I liked him. But Don was an actuary by training. His skill set lay more in dealing with numbers than dealing with people. Don's focus was on finding ways to manage the insurance company to maximize profit. How do we make this more and more profitable and drive the stock price? Those were his marching orders from the top. Like everyone else on the new executive team, he had no experience whatsoever with a sales force like ours. They were used to running brokerages full of people who came in to work at their jobs every day.

But that wasn't what we had here at A.L. Williams. Our folks weren't people who saw themselves as working at a job. They were people who saw themselves as part of a *cause*. And you can't run a business like that as if it's an organization because it's not just an organization. It's an organism. It's something people are drawn to because they want to do something great with their lives. It's a *movement*. The day you start running it like an organization with org charts and lots of functions all neatly defined is the day it starts to die.

> This isn't just about business. It's about a living, breathing culture. It's about being part of a burning mission that people buy into and believe in with all their hearts.

And that's the reason I'm telling you this story—because it's not just true of A.L. Williams. It is a fundamental truth of leadership that applies to *any* business.

You can find companies with structures completely different from ours that understand that they are a group of people who are drawn together by the fact that they are all part of the same cause. That's one of the factors that made Apple great. The same goes for Southwest, Toyota, Zappos, and a thousand other companies, some famous and some no bigger than your local coffee shop.

If a computer company, an airline, an auto manufacturer, and an online shoe store (a *shoe* store!) can be driven by a powerful mission, then *any* company can find and champion that kind of mission. This isn't just about business. It's about a living, breathing culture. It's about being part of a burning mission that people buy into and believe in with all their hearts.

What Art had created in A.L. Williams was a movement to transform the life insurance industry from being something that took advantage of people to being a force for good. He wanted to make a company that did good things for families and changed people's lives for the better.

Sandy's enthusiasm notwithstanding, the people from New York did not really grasp how central to the company's existence this mission was. Because of that, they did not fully appreciate the role Art had played in the company's operation. They saw him as a great sales leader and motivational speaker, but certainly not essential to the company's success. Sure, they figured, there'd no doubt be a few bumps in the road during the transition, but we'd all get along fine without him. What they didn't realize was that our field wasn't going to behave like your typical sales force of full-time "professional" salespeople. And Art wasn't just the founder. He was the electromagnet at the heart of the thing. Cut off the current and the whole thing would start to drift apart.

When I talk to stock analysts and other professionals in the finance world, it floors me how they just cannot get the concept at the center of how our business works. I tell them to picture a health club.

Every January, everybody in the country says, "I'm tired of being a fat tub of goo. I am *not* going to be the chubby old me of last year. I'm going to get in shape." Then they all go out and join a health club. For about a month and a half, you can't find a machine that doesn't have somebody on it. By April you could shoot a cannon through the place and not hit a soul. Why? Because it's *voluntary*. If their boss said, "Your fat tail needs to lose twenty-five pounds in the next six months, or you're fired," they'd be down there on the treadmill every day. But their boss doesn't say that. And in our company, the salespeople don't even *have* a boss.

These people are not W-2 employees. They're 1099 folks, independent contractors. That means nobody can tell them what to do. They aren't *hired*. They *join*. It's a volunteer army. They didn't come here for a job, and they sure didn't come here for a boss. They're here to be independent. They don't have to come to the meetings. They don't have to do *anything* if they don't want to.

Again, this is a fundamental truth of human nature that operates in *any* business. When a company's people stop being inspired, when they lose that crucial connection to the company's mission and start being just part of a work force, that company is in trouble. Even if all its vital signs still look good on the outside, if its heartbeat isn't strong then it's already on its way to the emergency room. In most companies, as long as people are on the payroll they at least keep going through the motions. In our company the impact is a little more dramatic and immediate because everyone in the sales force is there on a pure commission basis.

Here's how people join our business: They say, "I'm in."

Here's how people quit our business: They say, "I'm out."

That's it. When people quit, they don't notify anyone. They don't come into the office and announce that they're resigning the way I did at Life of Georgia. They just don't show up at the meeting next week. And that is exactly what was about to happen.

Ask the Right People the Right Questions

One day that summer, not long after our family outing for Picture Day, Don Cooper held a meeting in a giant conference room at the office for all the executives and management. I was sitting with my friend and colleague Chess Britt. Chess exemplifies the expression "still water runs deep." When he has something to say, I know I need to stop whatever I'm doing and listen. Over the years, Chess would become one of my anchors at the company and eventually run all of marketing.

Don was going through a presentation from the *Harvard Business Review*, describing what happens when companies go from the entrepreneurial phase to the established business phase. "When you go through that transition," he explained, "you'll go through some bumps, some little ups and downs. That's normal." He had a chart up there that showed the classic line of upward growth, with some little squiggly lines here and there showing the bumps in the road.

Chess looked over at me and in his wonderful dry way said quietly, "I think these lines may be a little more squiggly than he thinks they are."

Truer words were never spoken.

For the first few months, things looked like they might be okay. The numbers held through the early fall. By late fall, sales were slipping.

Remember, this is an all-commission sales operation we're talking about here. Nobody had any specific quotas they *had* to reach. In fact, strictly speaking nobody *had* to do *anything*. And in an all-volunteer sales force, if people aren't inspired to go out there and sell, they don't.

December was seriously down, but then, December is always a slow month. January came, and suddenly it was like everyone who was gone for the holidays *stayed* gone. By February, our sales numbers and the size of the sales force decreased by half. Those lines were getting squiggly, all right. We were dropping like a rock.

Strangely enough, it didn't look that way to the executives in New York due to a curious aspect of the insurance business. A lot of companies are cash-driven. If sales suddenly drop 50 percent, then earnings drop 50 percent. But that's not the case in our business because an insurance company has a huge book of in-force business, which defers a lot of your costs early on. This meant that even though our sales force was collapsing and new sales weren't happening, earnings at the company were not down dramatically. To Sandy and the rest of them up in Manhattan, it didn't look like the disaster it was.

My vantage point was different. While they saw things in terms of impact on earnings, I saw things in terms of impact on the field. I was in charge of compensation to the sales force. And suddenly there wasn't any compensation to be in charge of.

The way our business works, we advance commissions to the agent on new sales when they happen. When you write a sale, we collect one month's premium from the new customer and put them on a monthly automatic bank draft for their ongoing premium payments. Meanwhile, we advance nine months' worth of commissions to you, so that you get significant compensation for the sale right away. In effect, this creates a loan against your account, which then earns out over the course of the next nine months as the monthly premium payments come in. This was a revolutionary idea for the insurance business. Plus we were advancing new commissions not just once or twice a month but twice a *week*, so that our people were getting a constant flow of immediate cash-in-hand rewards for their efforts. This was another Art Williams innovation. This created a debit balance, which would normally be earned back by future premium payments as well as by additional new sales.

Now, with sales dropping so dramatically, suddenly there were barely enough new premiums coming in to offset the debit balances. That February, we had one pay period that actually amounted to a net chargeback, meaning that not only did the agents not get paid, but the "earnings" coming from their organization amounted to a net *negative*. Being in charge of compensation I could see the numbers, and I knew what was going on the moment it happened.

There were no checks going out.

If you woke me up in the middle of the night by blowing a Klaxon horn and shining a 10,000-watt light in my face and shouting at me, "Addison! Explain in complete detail exactly what the people at the top of this thing need to watch in order to run this company effectively!" you'd get an immediate response. I wouldn't have to think, I'd just blurt out four words:

"Checks to the field!"

That's it. The earnings and commissions going to the members of the sales force are the life blood of the organism. If checks are going up, life's okay. If checks are going down, life's not okay. It's really that simple. And right now, checks weren't just going down, they were *gone*.

But up in New York, they didn't see that. They were using the conventional metrics to assess the state of things. The conventional metrics weren't giving them the right answers. The troops on the ground knew we were in trouble, but the generals weren't asking the troops.

I knew this was bad. If we didn't get some cash flow going out to these guys, they were *all* going to quit. There'd be nobody left. Once again, I wasn't sure how much longer I'd still have a job. Only this time, it wasn't because I thought I might get fired. It was because I wasn't sure how much longer we'd still have a company.

By this time, our family had settled well into our little three-bedroom ranch house in Snellville. In fact, Loveanne had just ordered a new entertainment unit for our den, with a place for our TV, stereo, and bookcases.

I called and cancelled the order.

Sometimes You Have to Be the One Who Speaks Up

That month Sandy came down to Georgia to have a meeting, a sort of review-of-the-troops to see how things were going. He brought his two right-hand guys with him, a man about my age named Jamie Dimon and another gentleman named Bob Lipp, who was Sandy's most trusted lieutenant. Today Jamie Dimon runs JPMorgan Chase. Bob Lipp eventually became the CEO of Travelers Insurance. Me and a handful of other guys who'd been around a good while were brought in.

So there I was, in the room with Sandy, Bob Lipp, Jamie Dimon, and some other top executives. Sandy was sitting at the head of the table, chewing on a cigar, going around the room and asking each one in turn how he saw things. Were things getting better, were things improving?

Now they *were* asking the troops on the ground. What would the troops say back?

Sandy is a brilliant, self-made man, and he can be a very intimidating presence. A lot of jobs had been cut when New York took over. The A.L. Williams veterans in the room were as worried about their own necks as they were about anything else. Nobody was about to go negative in front of Sandy. One by one, everybody was saying things like, "Well, it's been challenging, but I really think we've made a lot of the right moves, and things are going better, blah, blah, blah." People talked about what projects they were working on, how they saw things improving in their particular area, and so forth. It was coming around to me. I was sitting there thinking, "Oh, this isn't going well."

Finally Sandy got to me. "John?" he said. "How do things look to you?"

What was I supposed to say?

In the half-year since Sandy's team had taken over the company, there'd been this feeling around the office that these Wall Street guys were coming in and saying, "Here, let us show you country bumpkins how a *real* business is run." I didn't get the feeling that any of these guys were going to take too kindly to this particular country bumpkin telling them their business. But I just couldn't see sugarcoating things. There's a time for diplomacy and a time when you have to put caution aside and be candid. I knew this was one of those times. I figured this might be my last chance to have any influence here.

It was that fork-in-the-river thing again. When you see the path ahead of you dividing, all you can do is take the direction that looks and feels like the right one and trust that consequences will sort themselves out.

> There's a time for diplomacy and a time when you have to put caution aside and be candid.

Okay, I thought, *here goes.*

"Look," I said. "With all due respect, the situation here's not bad—it's worse than bad. It's a disaster."

As I pulled out a few pieces of paper I'd brought in with me, I still remember the silence that rolled around that conference table like a blanket of fog socking down an airport. I briefly ran down the numbers and walked through how things had crashed in the past six months.

"The bottom line is," I said, "we've got no checks going out. I don't know how long these folks are going to hang in there

with you all, but if they're not getting a check, it won't be long."
I set my papers down, looked around the conference table, and
summed up with an image that had been running through my
mind for days.

"Guys," I said, "this thing is on fire. It's burning. It's the
Hindenburg at Lakehurst."

For a moment, there was that dense fog of silence again. I
couldn't read anyone's expression. Then there was some more
talk. Before long the meeting broke up. As we left the room, the
guys from New York were all murmuring to each other.

Well, I thought, *what's done is done.* Had I opened my big
mouth and put my foot in it up to the knee? Maybe I *would*
get fired after all, regardless of whether or not the company
pulled through.

The next day, I got a phone call from New York.

"John?" asked the voice. "Jamie Dimon."

Oh boy, I thought, *here it comes.* I figured the chances were
good I'd be clearing out my desk right after this phone call.

I said "hello" back.

"Listen, John," said Jamie, "I just want to thank you for
being so honest and for being the guy in the room who spoke
up and told us how you really see it."

Apparently they'd talked after the meeting and decided that
maybe this guy from Georgia had a ticket on the clue bus. I was
not being fired. Even better, I was being listened to.

That right there is one thing that sets leaders like Jamie apart
from the rest: not only asking the right questions of the right
people, but also *listening to the answers.*

About a week later, Bob Lipp came to Atlanta to have an
emergency strategic and tactical session with a handful of us.
Bob started out at Chemical Bank in his twenties as a teller and
worked his way up to president before being tapped by Sandy to

help create what was at this time the rapidly expanding empire of Primerica Corporation. Bob is a wonderful human being, brilliant businessman, and remains a very good friend to this day.

Bob met with me, my boss, and a few other long-timers, and we suggested some ideas about things we'd tweak with compensation. We knew we had to infuse some excitement into the sales force. At the moment, the only thing that was going to produce excitement was a little cash. We came up with an idea to create a bonus system without doing a lot of damage to the company's bottom line, something based on monthly production that would put more money in our reps' hands.

About that same time Sandy sent a new CEO down to Atlanta to run things. Pete Dawkins had an unbelievable reputation. As a highly decorated Vietnam veteran and Army general, Rhodes Scholar, and Heisman trophy winner, Pete was a Renaissance man and the picture of an American hero. Having him on board was a great injection of much-needed inspiration to the sales force.

Once he was in Duluth and working with the company, it was obvious that his reputation was well deserved. Pete had tremendous integrity, character, and energy. He and his wife Judi threw themselves into the task of reinvigorating the company and for the next months they were flying around the country doing a ton of work with the field.

Between the innovations we brainstormed in that emergency meeting with Bob Lipp and Pete and Judi's hyperkinetic activity, things at A.L. Williams slowly began to stabilize. It wasn't as if we started seeing strong new growth or anything like that. But at least that sickening downward plunge slowed and stopped. We were pretty sure we were no longer heading straight for the ocean floor.

Still, we'd taken on a lot of water. I didn't know if we could bail fast enough or hard enough to stay afloat long.

Don't Let Your Job Description Define You

The new challenges kept on coming. Later that year, Primerica changed the name of our agency. A.L. Williams became Primerica Financial Services. Suddenly, for the first time since the company was founded, our name was gone and our people had a new identity.

For some of our folks, this was actually an exciting thing. We were now part of a Wall Street giant, which added a sense of big-league credibility to our business. For others it was a huge negative, especially for those people who'd been around for a long time and considered themselves A.L. Williams to the core. For these people, losing the name A.L. Williams was almost like losing Art all over again.

The name change also made an enormous amount of fresh work for me. Changing a company name sounds simple enough. You just change the name, right? Of course, it's a whole lot more complicated. Just on the level of pure logistics, all your materials have to change—your forms, your bank accounts, all your legal documents—everything. For us, though, it was even more complicated because we had a whole licensing process in every state, unique to each state. For months afterward, I was traveling all over the country, making sure that we had our name change done legally and completely in each state.

Meanwhile, back at the home office, the executive team was scrambling to get a handle on field morale and find a new path back to the kind of growth we'd had in the past.

That summer, the summer of 1992, we were going to hold a big convention in Fort Worth, Texas. Everyone knew this was going to be a critical moment. It would be our first convention since Art left and we had gone from being A.L. Williams to being Primerica Financial Services. How well it came off, or didn't come off, would have a huge impact on field morale.

In most companies, conventions are a nice break from the routine. Honestly, they don't have a heck of a lot of impact on the normal operation of the business. They can be boring or a lot of fun, depending on the nature and culture of the company. Either way, they are basically an extracurricular thing, like a paid vacation. For a company like ours, conventions are practically the heartbeat of the business. They are a time for people to renew their passion and commitment, their visceral sense of why they're here doing what they're doing. It's something like plugging in your cell phone to recharge its battery. Every now and then you need to plug in the field so they can recharge.

In our business, we have an expression: "Leaders are born at events." Not only that, momentum is born at events. People come away from the convention saying, "Oh, right, *that's* who we are!" There are always a good number of people at an event who get so fired up that they make a powerful renewed commitment to their businesses. For our folks, going to convention isn't a vacation. It's a pilgrimage. Like a convention for a major political party, it defines who we *are* at that point in our history, and its impact can last for months and even years.

When Art was still there, our conventions were virtually a one-man operation. He had people who ran things for him, but Art knew what he wanted to do with an event and he knew how he wanted to do it. He knew how to pace the thing, how to paint an inspiring picture for people, and create huge excitement. Art is a man who knows how to put on an event and make it a memorable, even life-changing experience. But Art was long gone, and neither Pete nor anyone else on the executive team had the faintest idea how any of that convention magic worked. They were used to boring corporate conference-style events. There were a lot of different opinions and viewpoints about what should happen at that convention. I wound up being pulled into one of those meetings with Pete and his top people as they were trying to figure out what to do.

A few months earlier, Sandy had sent an executive named Marge Magner down to Duluth to pull together a small team to work with her on focusing the company's marketing and message. Because of my little "Hindenburg at Lakehurst" speech I was one of the people selected for that group. Marge later wound up running the global consumer business for Citigroup. These days she's a major player in the world of private equity. Marge put me in front of Pete to share my views about where we were off track in our message and what we needed to be focusing on. Now I had been brought in to help advise Pete on how to put together this convention.

Just as when I'd been pulled into meetings in the mid-eighties to help collect marketing data for Art, this was way above my pay scale. I oversaw compensation and licensing. Nobody involved in planning events reported to me. I was nowhere near the C-suite level as were the others in the room. But hey, if they wanted to hear what I thought, I'd tell them.

After listening to them talk about their ideas for a while, I said, "I've got to tell you, if you do what you're describing, they're all going to either go to sleep or stand up and walk out. That just isn't gonna fly."

I started outlining a few ideas and ended up helping them organize the event and working closely with Pete on the content and overall message of his talk.

We all approached Fort Worth with a great deal of trepidation. There was still an enormous amount of feeling in the field that we had never recovered from losing Art and perhaps never would. While some were excited about moving forward, there were many who still mourned the "good old days" of A.L. Williams and who had a pretty strong my-arms-are-folded attitude about the new regime. There was a huge undercurrent of allegiance to the past and a sense that the jury was still out on whether this "Primerica thing" was really going to work or not.

Happily, the convention came off well after all. Maybe not the kind of knock-your-socks-off event we'd have had if Art were there, but still a success. The mere fact that it hadn't bombed served as something of a calming, stabilizing force. People started saying, "Okay, maybe this thing isn't going to go out of business after all. Maybe we have a chance here."

After Fort Worth, Pete and the other top executives started relying on me as the behind-the-scenes guy helping design the events and craft the message. Pete took to having me work with him every week on his TV broadcast to the field. Without intending to, I was more or less gaining control of the message apparatus of the company.

Was this part of my job description? Not even slightly. It wasn't the reason I'd been hired in the first place. It wasn't what I'd been trained to do, and it wasn't what my nominal position called me to do. But it needed doing, and I was the one who spoke up and showed up.

Close Your Eyes, Pray, and Jump

Growing up, I had no particular interests or skills that pointed in any clear career direction. In school, I was always a good student, but there was no specific area where I excelled or had a clearly defined skill set. In this way, I was very different from my father.

Dad was, and is, one of those incredibly handy guys who can fix anything. Anytime something needed replacing, repairing, or building from scratch, Dad could do it. He could draw as well as any draftsman or architect. He has a beautiful singing voice and often sang solos in church. He is so talented in so many ways.

I inherited none of that. My skill set, if you want to call it that, is about as opposite from my dad's as you could get. I am dangerous with a power tool. I couldn't carry a tune if you put it in a bucket and handed it to me. I've never been very creative or versatile or talented, the way my father is. As much as I love him, I did not take after him much. I take more after my mom, with her voluble, sociable, personable style, and who may have been the only person on earth with a worse singing voice than me.

There was one time, though, that the hint of a specific ability briefly poked its head out, like Punxsutawney Phil's snout on a cloudy Groundhog Day. I didn't grasp its value or significance till many years later.

In fifth grade one of our teachers, Miss Harper, assigned us each to do an oral book report on the biography of a famous person. Later that year, we all did another report. I chose Rockefeller. For this first report I was assigned the task of reading a book about Napoleon Bonaparte and preparing a 20-minute oral report on his life.

One Thursday a few weeks later, I was sitting in class. My mind wandered wherever it went. Miss Harper was up there talking. Suddenly I heard her say, ". . . and now Mr. Addison will give us a twenty-minute report about the life of Napoleon. Mr. Addison?"

You ever get that feeling where your gut just sinks down to your feet?

I just don't think in a linear way. My brain heads off in this direction and then that direction. Sometimes you just can't tell *where* it's headed, and neither can I. As I said, when I speak I never use a script. It just wouldn't work. Instead, I handwrite all my notes on sheets of paper in big bold letters. Sometimes I end up using those notes. Other times I head down a completely different path. Organization is not an item on my inventory of personal strengths.

So there I was, frozen in my desk, Miss Harper's words reverberating in my ears. Me being me, I'd thought that book report was due the following Thursday. Not *this* Thursday. Not today. Had I read the book yet? It's fair to say I'd *started* it. Did I have anything prepared? Absolutely nothing.

Oops.

It seemed to me, I had two choices. I could stand up and say, "I'm sorry, Miss Harper, I'm just not ready. I messed up and wrote the due date down wrong." But Miss Harper was old school about things like getting your work done on time. I knew that option wouldn't go over well. Which left the only other choice: close my eyes, pray, and jump.

Story of my life.

Okay, I said to myself, *let's do this.* I got up from my desk and marched up to the front of the classroom, then turned around and faced the class. Miss Harper was over to my right looking at me expectantly.

I knew how it all started. I knew he was born in Corsica and rose to power during the chaos that followed the French Revolution. I was also pretty sure about how it ended. There was a battle at Waterloo that he lost, and then he got exiled and died. All I had to do was fill in a bunch of stuff in the middle. In my ten years on the planet, there must have been at least a few tidbits of information about Napoleon, or France, or the nineteenth century, or *something* relevant, that had seeped into my head and stayed there. Right?

So, I talked. I have no idea what I said. After I'd finished, I sat down. A moment of silence hung over the room. Then Miss Harper spoke up. "Mr. Addison," she said. "In 25 years as a public school teacher, that's the best oral book report I've ever heard."

As I sat back in my seat a distinct thought went through my mind: *Hey, that's gotta be good for something.*

I'd had a lot of fun up there, talking to the whole class like that. I hadn't been scared. I'd had a blast. I may have been disorganized and nowhere near as prepared as I should have been. I may not have had a clue what I was going to say as I stood up and turned to face the class. But, I *connected* with that roomful of kids. By the time I sat down again, they all knew who Napoleon Bonaparte was.

As a 10-year-old, I didn't see how that could possibly be useful. I knew it meant something, but what? Not the faintest idea. So I filed the thought away somewhere in my brain and forgot about it.

At three and a half times that age, I knew *exactly* what it meant.

In early 1993, the executive team was planning a meeting in Atlanta with our top sales force leaders to introduce some product modifications and a change in the compensation structure. In the balance, these were going to be very positive improvements for the field, but they were not simple changes and would take some explaining. The mood among the field leadership was not great. This wasn't going to be an easy thing. Once again, I was pulled into a meeting with Pete, Ed Cooperman (whom Sandy had recruited from American Express), and some of the other top executives.

They'd brought in a gentleman to run marketing named Doug Martin. He was now my boss and was working with Pete on how to present the changes. As the discussion went on and on, at one point Pete turned to me and said, "John, how would you do this?"

I stood up and went through it. "Okay, here are the points I would emphasize. Here's what I would say, and here's what I wouldn't say." After I'd been going on for a few minutes, Pete and Ed looked at each other, then back at me.

"John," said Pete. "Why don't *you* do this?"

Why don't *I* do it? *Me?*

Today, speaking to an auditorium full of people and connecting with folks at a heart level is one of the greatest joys of my life. But at this point, the only speeches I was giving were to our offices that were undergoing changes in their licensing laws. Those little speeches, if you want to call them that, were not even remotely motivational or inspirational talks. They were, "Okay, guys, here's what's changed, here's how you gotta do it, here's what's going on." I'd sprinkle in a few humorous stories here and there, to keep things fun. That's all. So yes, I'd stood up in front of little groups and done some speaking—but nothing like this.

Still, I had developed a strong relationship with the sales force leaders. They knew I was a guy they could call if they had a problem and that I'd do my best to get it fixed for them. I knew that, at the very least, we'd have some rapport and they wouldn't laugh me off the podium.

We held the meeting with about 200 of our top income earners, who were also our senior field leaders. These folks were the key opinion shapers in the field, the guys and gals on the front lines of battle. Whenever the rank and file was having a hard time, senior field leaders were the people they came and talked to about it.

Everyone knows the stereotype about the path to success in corporate America. The way you reach the top, so the idea goes, is to claw your way up there by pushing down and climbing over others. I can't really comment on how true that is in any other business, or whether it's true at all. What I can say is that in our business, the *only* way you get to the top is by pulling a whole lot of other people up with you. This meant that the little group of people sitting in that hotel conference room wasn't just a collection of 200 individuals. It was 200 men and women who were carrying into the room with them the hopes, dreams, challenges, and bitter frustrations of tens of thousands of people.

As we got started, the atmosphere in the room was not the most relaxed. These people's organizations had been through a lot of heartbreak the past few years, and their expectations for the meeting clearly were not positive.

After a brief welcome and stage-setting from Pete, I was introduced to give the details. I walked up to the podium, turned to face the group, and talked for the next forty-five minutes.

I started by walking through the details of the changes we were making and why. Then I told them how I saw these shifts, what they would mean to the field, and how I believed they would help change things for the better. I talked about how much I loved our company, about what it stood for, and what it meant to me. I just talked from my heart about our company and what we were doing in the world.

> The *only* way you get to the top is by pulling a whole lot of other people up with you.

The presentation got a tremendously positive response from the leadership. For a lot of these guys, all they'd been hearing, day after day, was their people coming to them and telling them how stupid we were at the home office, how we didn't get it, and what a mess we were making of everything. Some of them told me later that this meeting was the first time they started thinking, "At last there's someone there who speaks the same language we do!"

After the meeting, we had dinner with the group. During the evening Bob Safford, one of our top field leaders, came over to me and said, "John, I was sitting out there today in that meeting, watching you the whole time. And let me tell you, I believe I was seeing the future CEO of our company."

I didn't know about that, but it was clear that my visibility had increased with the corporate leadership. Sandy was there and didn't miss the fact that our guys had responded to my talk in a way that they hadn't responded to any other talk since Art had left. It wasn't brilliant, and it sure wasn't Art. But it had had a strong impact and a positive one. They saw that I wasn't just a behind-the-scenes idea guy. I'd had an impact on these people. I could communicate with them in a way that made a difference to the organization.

That meeting proved to be a significant event for Primerica, one that went a long way to help stabilize things and bolster more confidence in our long-term prospects among the field leadership. For me, it was a pivotal moment in my career. Whether it was planned or not (and of course, it wasn't), something critical had happened.

I'd found my calling.

Focus on Your Strengths

There's a passage in the Bible that says, "Train up a child in the way he should go, and when he is old he will not depart from it." (Proverbs 22:6.) But exactly what is that "way he should go"?

A lot of parents interpret this passage to mean that you should raise your kids in a strict way, following the path you set for them, being well-behaved, doing all the things you as parents believe they should do. But that's not really what it means. If you study it in the original Hebrew, what Solomon is saying is not to teach your child to be a good person, or to be obedient, or anything like that. He's saying, find in that child what his or her unique talents are. Train your children up in the way *they* should go—not necessarily in the way *you* *think* they should go.

Loveanne and I have two great boys. Both of them are wonderful kids. They couldn't be more unlike each other. Our oldest son, Kyle,

> Being a real leader doesn't mean you're the one who knows how to do it all. It means you're the one who knows how to *get it done.*

has always been very mathematically inclined and turned out to be brilliant with computers. He works for the company, managing all kinds of gizmos I can't even comprehend. He built the computers I use in my office. Tyler, our youngest, has just finished law school and now works at Primerica on state government relations. He's a words guy, not a numbers guy. They both found their paths, and their paths are totally different.

Every tree is going to try to grow toward the sun, but as they do, some will lean this way, some that way. Each one finds its own unique pattern of growth. Children are the same way. As a parent, your job is to be a student of your children and help them find what they're naturally good at. To help them find that unique spark within them and fan it into full flame.

As a person, it's your job to do that for yourself too.

You don't have to be talented and skilled at everything to be a great leader. In fact, you can't be talented and skilled at *everything.* Nobody is. Being a real leader doesn't mean you're the one who knows how to do it all. It means you're the one who knows how to *get it done.* Two very different things. Being the one who knows how to get it done *always* means working together with the talents and skills of others.

Real leaders aren't excellent at everything. But they do have to be excellent in their own personal area of strength, whatever that may be.

If you want to be a successful leader, you need to figure out what you're good at, and then do it. I know that sounds ridiculously simple, but it's amazing how many people don't ever do it. Way too many people spend way too much of their time and energy working to improve on things that they're frankly just not very good at but *wish* they were good at. Here's a formula for success: Find something you're good at without trying hard—and then try hard.

The truth is that all people are *not* created equal. In a free society, they should all be equal under the law and should all have the same rights. But people themselves are not all equal. They're all different. Everyone is born with their own strengths and weaknesses. I could try for a million years and never do what Michael Jordan does in basketball, what Peyton Manning does in football, or what Blake Shelton does in concert. You could send me to Julliard for twenty years to work on that singing voice of mine, and I'd still scare away the wildlife.

I'm not saying you shouldn't try to get better at those things you're not good at. I'm not saying you should use "Oh, that's not my area" as an excuse to be incompetent at basic skills that everyone needs to get around in life. But in an area that truly is not your strength, no matter how hard you work at it, the best you'll ever be is mediocre. If you focus on the things you have natural ability at and work on those, then you've got a chance at being great—or at least, being great at *something*.

Everybody's good at something. Everyone has some distinct talent or area of potential excellence. What's yours? If you don't know, make it your business to *find out*. You have to develop a good understanding of yourself, of who you are, what you're good at, and honestly, what you're not good at and will never be good at. Most people are incredibly good at lying to themselves. You have to look at yourself with complete honesty.

Maybe you're a great parent, good with your kids. Maybe you're good with people. Maybe you don't see yourself as very brave, but you're caring and thoughtful. Maybe you're great at being organized. Maybe you're funny. Maybe you're serious. Maybe you can sing. Make a list of every ability and positive attribute of character you can think of.

What motivates you? Are you a good communicator? Are you a good listener? Good with numbers? Good with animals? Good with your hands?

Forget about the "not very good ats" and focus exclusively on the "good ats." Every one of us has things we were put here on this earth to do. If you don't already know what *that* is for you, then find out, and focus on *that*.

When I gave that little talk to that group of 200 leaders in Atlanta, I was 35 years old. It had taken me that long to figure this out for myself.

Over the years leading up to that moment, I'd put an awful lot of energy into trying to be better at stuff I would *never* be good at.

Back when I was first in college, I got books on how to be organized. I went to a Franklin Covey Planner seminar to learn how to master time management and get all my tasks and priorities lined up and in order. Set 'em up, check this one off, move that one forward. Brilliant idea. All I ended up with was a planner full of yellow sticky notes that I never used. Linear organization simply is not one of my strengths.

Right now, I'm sitting at my table with folders all spread out in front of me, filled with half-written-in notebooks. Pages with notes for my talks, in no particular order, and when I say "notes" I don't mean a sequential outline, I mean a constellation of single words, topics, and phrases that to anyone else would look like a jumble of chaos. This is how it always is when I'm working on a speech. I'll start writing words and pretty soon I have pieces of paper spread out all around me. It's not actually a mess. It all makes sense. Just not a linear, classic-logic kind of sense.

I've spoken at events where I see the other speakers reading their script from a teleprompter. I have no concept of how that can possibly work for them. I can't do this with a computer. And I sure don't want a printed-out script. I just need a stand for my handwritten sheaf of papers and thoughts, and I'll go from there.

I am the textbook definition of disorganized. I work in spurts. I have projects I fuss at for a while, and then I move on to something else. Maybe I'll come back to it later, and maybe I won't. (And I was planning a career as a "management consultant" and "efficiency expert"?)

Going through college, I knew I loved history, economics, and philosophy. I went on to get my business degree. But even then, I honestly had no clue what I was going to do. How could I? I still hadn't sat down and figured out where my strengths lay.

One thing I did *not* do in college was join the extemporaneous speaking society or the debate club. I didn't have the slightest thought about going into public speaking.

Yet it's something that just comes to me naturally. I grew up in a little country town with gregarious, outgoing parents, in a community full of people like my uncle, A.W. Dalton. He was a classic Southern raconteur. A.W. and Aunt Lois lived just down the road from us and were part of the family. His story-telling wit and fun-loving style became an integral part of who I am. My strongest childhood memories are of going to Roy and Helen Moore's general store and listening to the old men sit around in chairs telling stories, with all their homey adages and folksy expressions and colorful colloquialisms, holding forth on any topic, for any length of time, to anyone who'd listen. There were *always* a bunch of *anyones* listening. Relating to people, getting up on a stage and story-telling, connecting with people? It's in my pores. I just never thought about it.

Never, that is, until the day in 1993 when I stood up in that Atlanta hotel conference room and talked to those leaders about how much I loved this company, and why, and where I saw us all going as we created our future together.

Yes, I had learned how to calculate the time value of money. I had that TI business analyst calculator and actually knew how to use it. I had my graduate degree and could read a business plan and pore over a spreadsheet if I had to. But those things were not my area of strength.

This was.

What I was good at was standing up in front of a bunch of people and getting a message across to them so that they got it in their bones and not just in their heads. I was good at knowing how they felt and what they needed to hear. I was good at speaking *to* them, not talking *at* them.

As I said earlier, luck happens. Or maybe it's really nine parts luck and one part fate. Or the other way around. However it works, events unfold themselves in your life. And it just so happened that I answered a newspaper ad for a "business analyst" and took a job with a company that turned out to be a leadership incubation system where public speaking was a central and revered part of the business. I had the opportunity to spend years working around Art Williams, as well as a bunch of our great leaders in the field, most of whom were tremendous public speakers themselves. I'd been able to study them, to figure out what they were doing and how they did it.

By the time I was standing up in that Atlanta conference room to talk, I didn't fully realize it, but I was ready.

I don't want to give the wrong picture here. It wasn't as if I was a polished, completely accomplished speaker right out of the chute. Like any skill, it was something I would have to work at for years to get better at it. That was okay. What mattered was that I was good enough at it to be able to bridge a delicate gap and help us make it through an incredibly difficult juncture we were at as a company.

It's a good thing it worked out that way because we were not out of the woods yet. Not by a long shot.

PRACTICE #3

Build on Your Strengths

Every one of us is born with our own unique talents and areas of potential excellence. The best you'll ever be at a weakness is mediocre. Why waste your precious time trying to do what others are already far better at? Instead, search out those areas where *you* have a natural proclivity, and then build on those.

* Find something you're good at without trying hard—and then try hard.

* As a parent, your job is to be a student of your children and help them find that unique spark within them and fan it into full flame. As a person, it's your job to do that for yourself.

* Don't let your job description define who you are and what you do. Sometimes you have to be the one who speaks up and shows up.

* Being a real leader doesn't mean you're the one who knows how to do it all. It means you're the one who knows how to *get it done*, which always means working together with the talents and skills of others.

ACTION STEP

Give yourself a natural-strengths inventory. Write out a list of everything you can think of that you are naturally inclined to be good at. Ask yourself, "Okay, what are my strengths, and what are my weaknesses? What am I naturally inclined to be good at?" Forget the "not very good ats" and focus exclusively on the "good ats."

CHAPTER 4

Anchors to Windward

Earn Your Position

He does not set out to be a leader, but becomes one
by the equality of his actions and the integrity of
his intent.

—DOUGLAS MACARTHUR

There aren't many people about whom you can say that the fate
of civilization genuinely rested on their shoulders. Winston
Churchill was one of those rare individuals. Churchill is remembered as one of the twentieth century's greatest leaders. That isn't
because everything was awesome and rosy and prosperous in the
U.K. when he was prime minister. It was one of the ugliest times
in that nation's history. At his moment of greatest leadership,
6,000 people a night were dying in the bombings of London. The
June 1940 "We shall fight them on the beaches, we shall fight
them in the hedgerows, we shall never surrender" speech and
all the rest of his great radio speeches, when he used his mighty
oratory to bring a terrified nation to its feet to fight the Nazis,
were conducted out of a tiny bunker, barely six feet by six feet.

Within the Cabinet War Rooms there's a little room called
the Radio Room. I've been inside that room. It's the most

claustrophobic thing you can imagine, more of a cubby than a real room. And Churchill was a large man. I love picturing him in that tiny, cramped place and terrible underground environment, with bombs going off above him, inspiring a nation to rise up against tyranny.

The space didn't exist for greatness. He *created* the space for greatness.

Leadership Abhors a Vacuum

The greatest opportunities for leadership typically arise in times and places where it's needed most. It is often those times when things are troubled or chaotic when you can move light years ahead—if you're the right person, if you're prepared, and if you're the one whom others trust and respect.

Nobody appointed Gandhi to embark on an effort to free India. Nobody gave George Washington a salary, a penthouse, and a pension during the tumultuous years leading up to the American Revolution and independence and said, "Okay, it's your job to be the one person everyone in this impossible situation looks to for leadership." People didn't trust Washington because he was president. He became president because people trusted him.

This is not just the story with great leaders like Gandhi and Washington. This is also how many of the most *destructive* leaders in history came to power: A vacuum existed, and nobody else stepped forward to fill it. Nature abhors a vacuum. If you don't fill it, someone else will, and they may not have the organization's long-range interests at heart as much as you do.

Real leadership is something that happens long before anyone appoints you or recognizes you as the leader. It starts by developing the ability to influence other people toward a goal, even when you're not their boss. It comes into being as others start saying, "You know this person is the one for the job." Having a title doesn't make you a leader. It may mean you have certain responsibilities, a specific job, or a certain salary scale, but the one thing it doesn't mean is that you're necessarily a leader. A title is only a title. Leadership is something you earn.

There will come times in your career when you can't just do what your job description says you're supposed to be doing. Sometimes, especially during times of hardship and confusion, you have to stand up and do whatever it takes to have a positive influence on the situation.

> Real leadership is something that happens long before anyone appoints you or recognizes you as the leader.

You can't always stand on the beach waiting for your ship to come in. Sometimes you have to swim out there and meet it.

Throughout the decade of the nineties, I did an awful lot of swimming. I just hoped we weren't going to sink.

Honor the Past, Look to the Future

By the mid-nineties, the initial terrifying collapse that happened when Art first left had slowed and stopped. Things had more or less stabilized. At the same time, Primerica was still highly vulnerable. We hadn't yet recovered from the trauma of all that drastic change, and for a lot of our people, it was hard to let go and move into the future.

When Art sold the company, there was a prevailing sense in both the home office and the field that our new corporate team represented almost a repudiation of the past. It was as if they were saying, "Okay, that was then, all that worked for you guys in the eighties—but you have to forget about all that because now we're going to show you how to *really* do this business." And of course, that doesn't work. You can't just toss out more than a decade of history and experience. These folks had deep roots in the past, and discarding or discounting the way things used to be felt personally like it was a repudiation of them and not just of their company.

During those early years of the new ownership, some of the people who'd been around a long time spent a lot of time and energy complaining about what the new people were doing. To be fair, there was a bunch to complain about. Their criticism and complaints were not necessarily wrong or without foundation. However, the simple reality was that things were never going to go back to the way they'd been.

There were people who, if they had their druthers, would roll the clock back, who couldn't seem to get out of the rut of regret and reminiscence. "Hey," they'd say, "remember that great meeting we had in 1984 . . . ?" A running joke at Primerica during those years was: How many people does it take to change a light bulb? Answer: Two—one to change the bulb and the other to stand there and say, "That's not how Art did it."

I don't believe in sitting around moaning about how everything used to be better in the good old days. Mostly when people do that, they're kidding themselves. Nostalgia's a fine thing. But let's face it, there's a lot about life in the "good old days," whichever good old days we might be talking about at any given moment, that wasn't all that good, and a lot that has since changed for the better. To my mind, that's the purpose of business: making the world a better place. We've been doing it for centuries, and sure enough, the world is a better place in so many ways.

When things are changing rapidly and feeling like they're veering out of control, you've got one of two choices. You can leave and go find something else to do. Or, if you believe in what you're doing, if you believe in the cause of the business, you can stay and find a way to help put things onto the right course. But you can't straddle the fence. You can't stay on but at the same time stay stuck in the rut of how things used to be.

It was a delicate equation. You couldn't say the company's first 13 years didn't matter. They mattered a lot. At the same time, it wouldn't work for us to live in the past either. We needed to build on that legacy, not stay mired in it. We needed to respect the past, operate squarely in the present, and focus wholeheartedly on the future. We *had* to move forward. If we didn't, we wouldn't make it to the new century.

Nostalgia and discontent among some members of the home office and sales force weren't the only problems facing us. We still had a major disconnect between the company itself and the people who were now at the top running it.

For a company with a huge, diverse, volunteer sales force spread out over 50 states, the relationship between the field and corporate team was already challenge enough. This relationship is not like the typical one between employees and management, or workers and bosses, or enlisted troops and officers. It isn't just a difference of position, authority, or role in the company. I don't know of anything else you can really compare it to. These people are independent representatives. In a field of thousands or even tens of thousands of people, each individual is running his or her own business. To someone used to a conventional command-and-control sort of corporate structure, working with a huge field of volunteer salespeople can feel like herding cats. Even in the healthiest of environments, it takes a lot of care and attention to make sure the two elements are hearing each other and that you're not letting friction get a foothold.

For us in the early nineties, it was that times a hundred. We had a field that had grown up organically with Art's football coach style and an executive culture straight out of the skyscrapers of Manhattan.

What's more, the messages coming down from that management kept shifting and changing on us. Sandy ran his businesses something like the way George Steinbrenner ran the Yankees. He'd throw a chief executive at it. If that guy didn't get the job done to Sandy's satisfaction, then by mid-season he'd pull that manager and put in another one. Throughout the nineties, while those of us in Duluth worked to keep things running smoothly, there was a fairly steady turnover at the top as Sandy replaced CEO after CEO. After Don Cooper we had Pete Dawkins, who helped us make it through that super-critical time in 1992 and 1993. But stepping into that position, at that time in our history, was like walking into a buzz saw. After Pete was there for a while, Sandy brought in Ed Cooperman, and so it went.

And it wasn't only a matter of turnover in the office of CEO. There were also constant changes in the composition of the executive team in general. Any time someone new stepped in, they naturally would want to have their own vision for the operation.

All of which meant that:

- We were being run from the top by people who, despite their good intentions, really didn't understand what made our operation tick.
- That group, their policies, agendas, and tactical goals, were in a state of constant flux.
- Underlying all of that, there was still a *very* strong current within the field of people missing Art and the "good old days," mourning the way things used to be.

The combination of losing Art together with total culture clash created a queasy environment of uncertainty that prevailed more or less right through the nineties.

See the World Through Other People's Eyes

The "freedom of choice" doctrine that brought Horace Johnson to join my class in Ficquett Elementary School in 1966 lasted another three years. In October 1969, the United States Supreme Court ordered the immediate desegregation of public schools. This put an end to the "all deliberate speed" doctrine that had been in place since Brown *v.* Board of Education and that had amounted to little more than ten years of foot-dragging and evasion. Now the schools had no choice. No more white schools and African-American schools and all that hogwash about "separate but equal." Now the schools had to get serious about integrating.

In Newton County they rearranged things so that the junior high classes, which consisted of grades eight and nine, would all be going to R.L. Cousins, which had been the region's African American high school. Newton County High School, which was the nearly all-white school, would now become the high school for everyone.

Not everyone was happy about this. Some of the wealthier white families got together and founded their own all-white private school. Similar schools sprang up in county after county. Clear across the South today you'll still find a swath of private schools that all say in their brochures, "Founded 1970." That's not a coincidence.

Sure enough, that year, the year I entered eighth grade, a lot of the white kids' parents pulled them from the Covington public school system and enrolled them in private school. My parents certainly had the means to pay the tuition. They weren't wealthy by any stretch of imagination, but my dad made good money at the mill and we were very much a middle class family. And a bunch of my friends were going there.

Not me.

Shortly before that school year began, my mom sat me down and said, "Look, son, I know you have friends going over there to that new school, and I know you want to be with them. But it's important to understand, the world is changing. You can't run and hide from a changing world. You've got to be part of it."

She was so right. With the benefit of hindsight, I'm so grateful that they kept me in the public high school. It was an adjustment, suddenly being with so many kids who were different from me. Having Horace as a friend was one thing, but that year our entire school population was suddenly about 50 percent African American. If you've ever seen the film *Remember the Titans*, you may have some sense of what it was like. The film is set at that same point in time and conveys exactly the same feeling and tensions as we saw going on at our school. In fact a lot of *that* film was shot in Covington, too. The final football scene takes place downtown at Homer Sharp Stadium, located right off the Covington town square.

I was now 13 and had a more conscious understanding of what was happening around me than I had when I was five and watched my mom insist on standing behind the woman in line at the grocery store, or even when I was nine and Horace joined our class at Ficquett. I quickly found that it was easy for me to get along with the new kids who were unlike me in so many ways and had come from a different world than mine.

> You can't run and hide from a changing world. You've got to be part of it.

I also soon realized that making this shift wasn't nearly so easy for many of my classmates. That was the year I began to understand that there are a lot of people in the world who are only comfortable when they're around others who are similar to them, who think like them and like the same things they like. When they're thrown in with those who are unlike them, it makes them uneasy.

In later years, I would also come to understand that being intolerant and judgmental is an enormous handicap in life. Not everyone is motivated by the same things you are or wants the same things you want. That doesn't make them wrong and you right. It just makes them different. If you're going to be successful, in business as in life, you have to be able to get along with people who are different from you, sometimes *very* different from you.

Probably the biggest thing I'd absorbed from my mom was how to put myself in another person's shoes, get a good sense of how they were experiencing the situation, and understand that it may not be at all the same way I was experiencing it. I learned the habit of trying to understand and appreciate the other person's perspective, even if I completely disagreed with it.

You can disagree without being disagreeable. When you do have disagreements, make sure it's over issues that matter, and not based on the ways you simply happen to have different preferences or a different viewpoint from the other person. As you work with different people, you'll find plenty of excellent times to keep your opinions to yourself. What my mother showed me was how to find the things we have in common, and move on past the places where we differ. Ninety-nine times out of a hundred, they just don't matter.

Out of all the challenges of that transitional time at Primerica in the nineties, the biggest was the company was dominated by two radically differing viewpoints. It wasn't about which one was *right*. From each of their perspectives, they were both *right*. It was about each embracing the other and all of us moving forward together. And clearly, that was not going to be easy.

The Power of Differences

During these difficult years, I started forming a close relationship with another guy who'd been there since the A.L. Williams days.

Back in 1982, when Gerald Tsai, the CEO of American Can, first bought PennCorp, he hired two bright young analysts to conduct his due diligence and help him be sure of what he was buying. One was Jay Fishman, who today is CEO of Travelers and one of the most respected financial individuals on Wall Street. The other was a young Wharton grad, a financial whiz kid named Rick Williams. When Sandy Weill came along and bought the company in 1988, Sandy and Jamie Dimon were so impressed with Rick that they were determined to keep him on board and find something big for him to do. When Sandy bought Art's agency in 1989, a strong chief financial officer in place was needed, so Rick relocated to Atlanta to serve as our CFO.

At that point, I was much further down in the origination's hierarchy than Rick was. I was one vice president among dozens, somewhere between mid-level management and upper-level management. Rick was much more senior than me. We interacted only occasionally, but I could see that he was financially brilliant. Far more importantly, he was also a solid guy with his head on straight.

One of our first real conversations happened in early 1991, at the point where sales had fallen off so steeply that we weren't sending any checks to the field and I was genuinely concerned about the company's survival. I went over to Rick's office one day, sat down, and said, "Hey Rick, I have to tell you, things are not good. We're not paying anyone anything. This thing is taking on water bad."

Rick was present at that "Hindenburg at Lakehurst" meeting a few days later, along with my boss, Rick Mathis, and Mike

Adams, our resident IT wizard. He was also part of that emergency meeting with Bob Lipp a week after that, where we came up with some immediate tactics to help stop the freefall. Out of those experiences, Rick and I started having regular conversations. The conversations weren't formal meetings—not set or formal, not on the calendar or anything like that. Rick would just wander over into my office, or I'd amble over to his, and we'd talk about things.

One thing that was clear right from the start was how different we were.

Rick has an almost superhuman ability to process and organize information. He is without a doubt the most organized person I've ever met. And while he's too polite to say so, I have no doubt that I am the most *disorganized* person he's ever met. When it comes to the numbers side of things, hey, I got a degree in economics. I have an MBA. I understand how income statements and balance sheets and all that stuff works when I have to. But the reality is that I would be terrible at his job or mediocre at best.

And Rick? I've seen him speak at our events many times and he always does a great job of it, but it's not something that comes to him naturally. He'll spend hours to prepare a 15-minute talk. With me, just wake me up in the morning and stick me up on the stage, and I'm good to go. I'm more comfortable in front of a few thousand people than I am around a conference table.

Rick is brilliant. I don't mean *kind of* brilliant. I mean *brilliant*. I don't care who's at the meeting. Rick is always the smartest person in the room. He is tremendously analytical and will listen patiently to every detail of every scenario. I'm more of a ready-fire-aim type of person. Sometimes he has to force me to sit down and listen.

In fact, in just about every way you could think of, we were different, which turned out to be one of our greatest strengths.

It's easy to surround yourself with people who all like the same things you like, listen to the same music, have the same political views, and share the same general skills as you. Ball players like to hang out with ball players. French horn players go out for coffee with other French horn players. Birds of a feather. . . . That's fine, but it will only take you so far.

It is critically important to surround yourself with people who are good at all those things that you're *not* good at. You need people on your team who complement your skill set, people who have a passion and a talent for those areas that leave you scratching your head. If you build on your own strengths *and* you have people in your life who are good people, people you like being around who have strengths that are the opposite of yours, then you've got a good chance of doing something far greater than you could ever have done on your own.

That's what started to happen with Rick and me. We couldn't be more opposite in how we approach a problem. Our personal styles, tastes, and professional skill sets are practically opposites of each other. Yet we not only complement each other, we also genuinely like each other and enjoy hanging around each other.

> It is critically important to surround yourself with people who are good at all those things that you're *not* good at.

Even with all those differences, it wasn't what was different about us that drew the two of us together. It was what we had in common. We *were* unlike in so many ways, but underneath all those superficialities of personality and style, we were very much the same in the ways that count most. Our shared vision for our company, which came out of our shared values, drew Rick and me together

No, he wasn't from Georgia. Yes, he was a northerner who grew up in New Jersey and went to Wharton, one of the most prestigious business schools on the planet. So you might assume he'd have come across as an outsider at the Duluth office. That short bio isn't the sum of who he is. Rick was raised on a dairy farm (There's more to New Jersey than Atlantic City!) and knew what it meant to work hard. He clearly was not some snooty prep school guy who believed his own press and thought he was hot stuff. He was sincere, honest to a fault, and one of the straightest shooters I'd ever met.

The thing I appreciated most about Rick was that he had figured the company out. He got who we were and what we were doing, both for families and for our sales force, and had quickly become a true believer in what we were all about. That, even more than anything about our particular personalities, was what drew us together.

There was also another force that drew us together during those years, a force larger than either one of us. As I said, nature abhors a vacuum, and so does leadership. It is especially during times of chaos and adversity when you may be called on to stand up and do whatever it takes to positively influence the situation. That was exactly the kind of vacuum Rick and I were drawn into together during the nineties.

Embrace Adversity

It's no accident this chapter started out with a few paragraphs about Winston Churchill. I'd always loved studying history, especially the lives of great men and women. I'd enjoyed reading about Churchill in college. During the late nineties and early 2000s, I really began delving into the details of his life and career. Primerica was exploring the idea of expanding into Europe during those years, and I was over in the U.K. a good deal. During those trips, I made it my business to visit and become familiar with all the major Churchill landmarks. Taking these trips helped give me a more vivid sense of his life and accomplishments.

There are many things I admire about the man, including the fact that he had so many personal hardships and strikes against him that he had to overcome to reach the position he did. The greatest thing about Churchill is that he served in a time of absolutely unbelievable difficulty and was able to face those trials and grow even greater within them.

Great leaders aren't remembered for what they do when everything's going along fine. Great leaders are remembered for what they do when things are tough, which is the same reason I also admire Thomas Jefferson, Benjamin Franklin, and their compatriots. The people who founded our country, our free enterprise system, and our Constitution bet it all. Most of them were wealthy men, landed gentry. They were doing well in America. It would have been very easy for them to just go with the status quo. But they risked everything, up to and including their necks, to found this country. It's those people, the ones who take a stand even when it's not convenient, who inspire me.

Real leaders don't accept adversity. They don't manage adversity. They embrace adversity. Challenging times are what they thrive on. In fact, the only way to genuinely survive adversity is to embrace it. Those who try to manage, side-step, or just wait out the bad times, typically don't make it.

> Great leaders aren't remembered for what they do when everything's going along fine.

During those first few years after Art left and the company went through such rocky times, Rick and I forged a sort of foxhole relationship. Before long that friendship had become a close bond. We not only liked each other, we also respected and trusted each other. Each of us viewed ourselves as protectors of the franchise, of what lay at the heart of the business and made it work. It was a good thing that we did because it needed protecting.

For example, the credit life insurance battle.

As part of our mission to help families gain control of their financial health, over the years we had broadened our product line to include a wider range of financial instruments. At the time our SmartLoan program, which Marge Magner had launched at the start of the decade, was growing strongly. SmartLoans gave you a way to use your home mortgage, wrap in your other debt, get a lower payment on the whole thing, and pay off your credit cards. It was a fantastic program, very helpful to the customer, very successful for the field.

Soon the word came down that New York was interested in seeing us add a credit life package.

The way finance companies work is if you take out a loan with them they also often sell you a specialized life insurance policy, called *credit life insurance*.

Such a policy is designed to pay off the loan in the event of your death. It's incredibly expensive and has a huge profit margin built into it.

It certainly wasn't hard to see why they wanted us to do this. "Hey, we've got this sales force and all these clients. We can sell all these other products to our clients too and greatly increase our profit per client." Credit life was a natural thing to want to add into the mix. It made perfect sense.

But not from the field's point of view. As far as our guys were concerned, they already sold life insurance. That was our core product line. They didn't need this credit life thing. They wouldn't like it, and they wouldn't want it. In fact, if we had added credit life onto the loans we were doing, our sales force would have gone ballistic. But because of the huge profit in it, there was constant push from New York for us to do it anyway.

This would have been a tough battle to fight on my own. But when it was Rick and me together, the head of marketing *and* the CFO saying the same thing, it lent our position a little more gravitas and commanded some attention.

We soon figured out that even with all the change happening around us, if the two of us were united on something, either both for or both against it, it was pretty hard for the executive leadership to go against us. What also helped was that Rick and I had both established a good amount of trust among Sandy and his top people. I don't know if they always liked what we said, but they knew we were honest and that we always had the business's best interests at heart.

The credit life insurance business was just one example of the things Rick and I were constantly battling to keep the ship from heading off in the wrong direction. We became ongoing strategic allies, helping to provide the company with some kind of constancy and course stability in the midst of all the storms.

There's a nautical term that works here. During a storm, if your ship is being blown off course and in the direction of something hazardous, you can drop anchors on the windward side of the ship, the side facing the wind, to stop the thing from running aground or getting wrecked.

Throughout the nineties, Rick and I served as anchors to windward.

You Don't Need a Title to Lead

When I started junior high school, my mom decided it was time for her to rejoin the working world. She took a position as a teacher's assistant at the local elementary school, which she did right up until I got married and started having kids.

She may have been *only* a teacher's assistant, but my mom often advised the school principal, Sam McGee. In a way, she quietly ran the place. At my mom's funeral in 2004, Sam told us all a story about one cold winter day. We don't get much snow in Covington, but on this day there was an especially big snowstorm. Sam lived in DeKalb County, way up toward Atlanta. It was close to an hour's drive from our little rural school on a good day, so it took him a good while to make his way in that morning. When he got there he found the school closed up tight as a tourniquet, with just a few staff people, including my mom, tying up a few housekeeping odds and ends.

Turned out, my mom had decided the roads were so bad that the school shouldn't even open, so she got the word out that school was shutting down for the day.

"Ruth, what in blazes are you doing?" Sam asked her.

"Well," she said. "These kids can't be out on those roads today, Sam. It's just too dangerous." And that was that.

Even though she never held any sort of position of authority, Mom was very influential in our little community. She wasn't wealthy, or politically connected, or in a place to wield any power. Title and position never seemed to be the point. Miss Ruth was who she was. People deferred to her because they trusted her. She had a great sense of humor and a strong moral compass. People found her incredibly easy to talk to. People would call her with their problems, sometimes telling her things they wouldn't tell anyone else. She would never judge them, just listen quietly and then give them advice. It was always good advice. I never once heard her say the word *hate*. She could talk to anyone and often did. I don't think I ever met a soul who didn't like her.

People will often wait to get into a leadership position before they lead. But you don't always have that luxury. Sometimes, especially if you're part of an organization that is struggling, you have to *create* your position. I found that happening at Primerica throughout the nineties. I was shaping the message at conventions for years before I was actually placed in charge of conventions. I developed my influence on marketing long before I was placed over marketing.

Leadership, at its heart, is more about influence than it is about position. Leadership is about learning how to be a force for the positive. If you want to be a leader, you have to *be* that leader before you have the title.

> If you want to be a leader, you have to *be* that leader before you have the title.

I know that all doesn't sound that hard. Not when it's just a bunch of words on a page. In the confusing, high-stress, moment-to-moment experience of reality in the trenches it can be excruciatingly difficult because sticking your neck out always comes with risk. The bigger the chaos and challenge of the times, the bigger the risk.

During those years Sandy and his team could easily have run out of patience with me and said, "Who is this loud-mouthed Southern guy with his noisy opinions? Get rid of him! Toss this guy out on the sidewalk!" And I mean, *very* easily. Sandy is not a shy man. You look at anyone who has achieved the kind of phenomenal successes he has, and you're not looking at a timid person. This is not a guy who is afraid to show the door to someone he thinks is getting in the way. Plenty of others in Duluth had been let go during the transition.

At the time, I don't think I fully appreciated just how far out on a limb I may have gone in some of those battles. I always tried to take an approach where I wasn't rude. I would be very strong in my opinions, but also do my best to act and speak in ways that would show people I still respected them. I was also careful to frame things in a way that wasn't threatening but would make it easy for others to say, "You know, he may be right." Still, I took some awfully risky positions.

It paid off. During those years I went through a series of promotions that reflected my increasing stature in the eyes of the executive team. From vice president of agency administration, I went to senior vice president, then executive vice president.

One day near the end of 1993, months after that that critical leadership meeting where I gave my first real motivational talk, we were in a meeting going over our budget for 1994, when my boss, the group vice president, was called up to the executive suite.

"John," he said, "Take over the meeting for me, would you? I'll be right back."

He wasn't right back. In fact, he never came back.

About 40 minutes later, I got called up to the executive suite too. There I was informed that I was now interim head of marketing. Within a month they dropped the "interim" part and made *me* group vice president.

While those earlier promotions were more or less incremental, this one was dramatic. All at once, I was in charge of events and conventions and running most of the company's marketing. I was regularly being brought up to New York to take meetings with our CEO and the executive leadership of our parent company.

For the first time, I now officially had the same level of stature in the company as Rick did. That was when our friendship really began to flourish as a partnership.

Sometimes negatives can turn out to be huge positives, depending on how you respond to them. When you're in a fairly comfortable environment, you're more likely to do just what you need to do to get by but never really grow to the extent that you're capable of. It's those times of the most chaos and the biggest challenges when you really have the ability to shine—if you see the moment, seize the moment, and are willing to make things happen.

It's not the circumstance; it's what you do about it. Sometimes what looks like bad luck is really just the adversity that allows you to flourish. Sometimes a situation that looks like the worst thing that could happen to your career can wind up being exactly the blessing your career needs.

How I responded when things were in terrible shape in many ways determined how I wound up where I did. During my first eight years at A.L. Williams, Art didn't really need me to take any kind of leadership role. If the company hadn't gone through the hard times it did after he left, I'd probably never have been anything more than a well-paid, mid-level executive taking care of his little corner of things. As it turned out, every new crisis worked out to push me higher.

When Art left the company in 1990, I was managing a department, a mid-to-upper-level manager among dozens of others. Over the next few years, I was moved up rapidly through the ranks to have a key executive position in the company.

And in 1995, I was promoted to president.

Don't Take Yourself Too Seriously

President. It sounds like a big deal, and in many ways it is a big deal. Everyone knows the story of Harry Truman and the sign on his desk, "The Buck Stops Here." That's a pretty good description of what my role became at this point. Everything that had to do with marketing, sales, our product offerings, our compensation and incentives, rewards and trips and events, conventions . . . all of it ultimately landed on my desk. If it had to do with the flow and management of finances and the company's financial statements, all roads led to Rick. If it had to do with anything else, those roads led to me.

Except that in some very crucial ways president is not quite as big a deal as it sounds. Being president of a company is not the same thing, for example, as being president of the United States. The president of our country is the nation's chief executive, the number one top decision-maker. This was not quite the case for me. Yes, I was president, and yes, I had a lot of decisions to make. But we also had a CEO.

Joe Plumeri, who had run Smith Barney for Sandy, was the CEO who promoted me to the position of president. Joe was one of the most memorable people I've ever encountered in my career. A true force of nature as CEO, Joe was a great speaker and was very hands-on in his executive role. He had very distinct and strong views on how he wanted things done. Having Joe there was like having Frank Sinatra as our CEO. Joe didn't simply have the title; like Sinatra, he just *was* the Chairman of the Board. He commanded authority simply by walking into the room.

Joe had run Shearson Lehmann's and Smith Barney's sales forces for years, and he knew the sales and brokerage industry inside and out. During his tenure at Primerica, Joe engineered a series of innovations aimed at professionalizing the operation. For example, he implemented our Financial Needs Analysis, a fantastic tool for assessing a family's unique financial situation that the sales force uses to educate potential clients and help them choose the products that serve them best. We'd had this tool for years, but under Joe we updated, modified and improved it, and made it center stage of our whole approach. Joe also brought in a lot of cross-selling of new products, including variable annuities and property and casualty insurance, which proved to be very successful products for us.

He also put in place a lot of compliance systems, which were crucial to bringing Primerica up to snuff in potential investors' eyes. When you have a company with this many salespeople, especially part-time salespeople, in the business of selling something as tightly regulated as financial services, one of the first questions investors will ask is, "How do you control this thing? How many things could go wrong with this many people selling financial services?" The compliance systems and other systemic improvements Joe put in place would prove invaluable for the long-term health and viability of the company.

On the other hand, they were not always easy for the field to absorb. Joe is not a hidden-agenda type of guy. You never had to say, "Gee, I wonder what Joe's thinking." He used to say, "If I'm coming at you, you'll see the trees moving." Sandy's decision to send Joe to Primerica was triggered, in part, by a negative article on the company that had recently come out in the *New York Times* and gotten a lot of visibility. The article had most of its facts wrong and was horribly unfair, but there *had* been a run of compliance issues in a few states. Sandy wanted Joe to come down and tighten things up, which he did. Whether his ideas and tactics did or did not ruffle the sensibilities of the sales force was not his top-of-mind concern.

That was my department. Joe had to make some tough decisions and knew that it might take breaking a few eggs to make this omelet. He counted on me to smooth the path and keep things stable whenever we hit any rough spots. During the years from 1995 to 1999, my title was president. For much of time, what I really did was serve as a human shock absorber. Glamorous? Not exactly. Possibly not what you'd think of when you hear the title *president*, but it was crucial to the health of the company. In the early nineties, I'd developed an ability to navigate between the sales force and the guys in New York. Now that became one of my chief functions.

Those years with Joe were crucial to my career, more so than I realized at the time. Joe helped me develop many of the skills and toughness I would need to see us through the difficult times coming a decade later. In time, I would have to become the rock against which other things broke. I would have to become a force of nature.

Mainly what the title of president meant was that I was working harder than ever.

Too often people think that getting into a position of leadership means that everybody else needs to feed them grapes and fan them while the work is getting done by

> When you're a leader, people need to see that no one is going to work harder than you, no one is more committed than you, and no one is taking more responsibility than you.

all the little worker bees. That's how a *boss* thinks—not how a *leader* thinks. There's a significant difference.

When you're a leader, people need to see that no one is going to work harder than you, no one is more committed than you, and no one is taking more responsibility than you. Real leaders aren't the ones who tell others what to do. Again, that's a boss. Leaders are the ones who inspire everyone else by their dedication, commitment, vision, and work ethic. Just because you *have* a title doesn't mean you don't have to keep earning it.

When you're in a leadership position, it's easy to start thinking you're a pretty big deal and that this thing is all about you. I hate to break it to you—but you're not, and it isn't.

I'll tell you who was a seriously significant person: Benjamin Franklin. The man discovered how to harness electricity, coauthored the Declaration of Independence, helped frame the Constitution, and for years brokered and maintained our fragile relationship with the European powers. Hard to say if this country would exist without him. All in all, a pretty important guy, right? And you know what? I've seen his grave.

The cemeteries of the world are full of irreplaceable people. Everyone is temporary. *Nobody* is that of a big a deal.

Quite often people who get into positions of leadership start thinking they're the center of the universe. Maybe the most important thing to understand, when you're a leader, is that *it's not about you*. It's about the enterprise. It's about helping the cause you're involved in go further.

At one point, a group of us were taking an overnight flight from New York to Nice on a company trip. On the flight with us was one of our top guys in our sales force, Bob Turley. Not only had Bob been one of the top-earning guys in our company since the early A.L. Williams days, but he was also a Cy Young recipient and World Series winner for the Yankees. Next time you're talking with a card-carrying Yankees fan just say the name *Bob Turley* and see what kind of reaction you get. Bob was the 1958 recipient of the Hickok Belt, joining the ranks of Rocky Marciano, Willie Mays, and Mickey Mantle. Bob is still the only athlete in history to win all three of these awards in the same year. If there was ever an athlete with a claim to celebrity status, it was Bob.

As it happened, Ringo Starr was also on this flight. Yankees fan or not, I'll bet anything you've heard of *him*.

We finally arrive in Nice, blurry from jet lag and less than perfect sleep. I'm at the baggage carousel with my team. Off to my left, there's Turley, hopping alongside the moving carousel, trying to schlep his bags off the thing, and off to my right there's Ringo struggling with his bag, trying to drag it off. Everybody's half asleep. I'm looking back and forth between the two of them, and I say to myself, "You know, *nobody's* that big a deal."

If someone tells you that you're a big deal, then that someone is either your momma (in which case she's right) or that someone is not telling you the whole truth. We've all got to pull our bags off the belt.

But here's who *is* a big deal: the team.

Bob Turley was a big deal because he was part of a team called the Yankees and A.L. Williams and Primerica. Ringo Starr was a big deal because he hooked up with a team called the Beatles. I was fortunate enough to become part of a team called Primerica.

There came a time later on, when the company was doing really well, when one of the top executives in New York asked me, "Hey, what kind of jet are you going to get now?" The truth was, with as much as I travel (I'm a three-million-miler with Delta) we could have easily justified the expense of having a company jet. But I never gave it a moment's consideration.

For one thing, I didn't want to send the wrong message to our investors. In some ways a plane is a terrible investment, and nothing says "executive extravagance" like having your own plane. I also didn't want to send a bad message to our own people, both our employees at the office and our sales force in the field.

Above and beyond those other reasons, though, I didn't want to send the wrong message to myself. I've watched people in business become successful to the point where they decide they need a jet, and a handler, a security crew around them, and all the other trappings of stratospheric importance. It's easy to lose perspective.

So, no, I never did get a jet. But I do travel a lot, and when I do I am typically picked up at the airport and driven around in a car the company rents. I love talking with these drivers. I try not to reinforce the gossip channel, but sometimes they'll tell me some pretty revealing stories about the celebrities and other highly important people they've driven around who behaved like complete jerks to them. Usually, at some point in the course of our ride, they'll tell me, "You seem like such a normal guy."

It's the highest compliment I can think of.

If you want to be an effective leader, it requires that you embrace a high degree of humility. Don't take yourself too seriously because as long as you do, no one else will.

One More Promotion

Throughout the nineties, as Rick and I deepened our friendship and worked to help keep the ship steered safely through its various sea storms, Sandy's financial empire continued to expand.

In 1993, Primerica bought Travelers, the venerable Hartford insurance pioneer (Travelers was founded the same year Abraham Lincoln won reelection), and Sandy took the name Travelers Group for the whole enterprise. At the time, there was a good deal of debate about whether we should become Travelers Financial Services. (Another potential panic in the field!) Good thing that didn't happen. At that point, the last thing the sales force needed was yet *another* shake-up in their identity. So while Primerica Corporation, the parent company, became The Travelers Group, we remained Primerica Financial Services.

> Don't take yourself too seriously because as long as you do, no one else will.

The Travelers merger was what brought us many new product offerings, such as Travelers variable annuity, and property and casualty. Notwithstanding the battles Rick and I had to fight over issues like credit life, this was an overall positive thing. We got new products, the company's stock went up, and since a lot of our senior sales force leaders were by now stockowners themselves, *their* stock went up.

In 1998, yet another round of ownership changes was under way. That year Travelers merged with Citibank, forming what would be known as Citigroup. With this new merger, Sandy had bitten off a seriously big chunk to chew on. The transaction resulted in a gargantuan operation that would take a ton of his and his people's time and attention to make it work smoothly. Another vacuum was about to be created.

The following year, as the decade came to a close, there was one more big change. In 1999 Joe Plumeri was tapped to run Citibank North America, leaving us once more in need of a new CEO for Primerica. This time, though, Sandy and the other top executives did something different. This time, they did not bring in a new executive from the outside to be put in charge of the operation. Instead, they decided the best thing for the company might be to let it be run by the people who were already there, people who knew the company from the inside and had for years.

On the eve of the new decade, Rick Williams and I were promoted together to co-CEO. From this point on, we would be sharing the chief executive's office and running the company ourselves.

The anchors to windward were now stepping to the helm.

PRACTICE #4

Earn Your Position

People often wait to get into a leadership position before they lead, but you don't always have that luxury. Sometimes, especially if you're part of an organization that is struggling, you have to *create* your position. You can't always stand on the beach waiting for your ship to come in. Sometimes you have to swim out there and meet it.

- The greatest opportunities for leadership typically arise in times and places where it's needed most. It is often those times when things are troubled or chaotic when you can move light years ahead. Sometimes a situation that looks like the worst thing that could happen to your career can wind up being exactly the blessing your career needs.

- Find people to work with whose skill sets complement yours. As important as it is to build on your own strengths, it is just as important to surround yourself with people who are good at those things you're *not* good at.

- Embrace adversity. It's where you have the greatest opportunity to flourish. Strong leaders thrive on challenging times. In fact, the only way to genuinely survive adversity is to embrace it.

- Real leaders are the hardest workers. When you're in a leadership position, people need to see that no one is more committed and working harder than you.

- Don't take yourself too seriously. If you do, nobody else will. No matter what your position is, you are not a big deal.

ACTION STEP

In your present business or career, is there a vacuum crying out to be filled? List at least three things you can do to serve the team that go beyond your job description

CHAPTER 5

Boom Years

Focus on What You Can Control

You have power over your mind, not outside events.
Realize this and you will find strength.

—MARCUS AURELIUS

In graduate school we had a wonderful teacher named T. P. Hall who taught us principles of leadership as well as the more nuts-and-bolts business of business. One day Professor Hall was talking to us about what it's like to be the leader of a large group.

"When you're at the top of an organization," he said. "You function like a big gear. Move even the slightest bit, and immediately you cause the next, smaller gears in sequence to move more, which in turn makes the even smaller gears move even more . . . and by the time you get to the lower layers of the organization you have hundreds or thousands of little gears all spinning furiously. All that frantic activity is all caused by that one, tiny movement you made.

"So here's the question: What happens if you keep changing your mind and moving in different directions?" He paused long enough for that picture to form itself in our minds, and then confirmed what we were already seeing: "That's right. All you're going to accomplish is to break the teeth off all the gears that are holding the whole thing up."

That was not a bad description of how the people of Primerica were feeling as we entered the new century. If Rick and I didn't want a lot of gears spinning like crazy and breaking off all their teeth, we knew we had to be extremely clear and consistent in our focus.

The question was: Focus on what?

Keep Your Hand on the Rudder

When you're the leader of any kind of organization, you have to be the most focused person on the team. This means you can't afford to let yourself be attracted to all the distractions. The further up some people get and the broader their responsibilities become, the more they lose focus on what the main thing is. They get a mile wide and an inch deep. Most people have the focus of an octopus on roller skates, a whirr of activity but no direction. You can't run a company effectively that way. If you're acting like a ping-pong ball in a wind tunnel, how are people going to follow you?

In every company, every organization, every project, every career, there are a hundred things you *could* focus on, and one or two things you *should* focus on. Those hundred things all seem important. They may even seem extremely important. But 98 of them are either secondary factors or things you can't really control. Those one or two key things are factors that can spell the difference between butting your head against a wall and surging forward, between failure and success.

> Most people have the focus of an octopus on roller skates, a whirr of activity but no direction.

If you want to lead a business effectively, you've got to focus your effort, energy, and time on what's going to produce results. There are some things you can change and some you can't. If I had one piece of management advice for leaders in charge of any organization, it would be: Find what you can control and focus on that.

This principle applies no matter what business you're in or what kind of group you're leading. If you want to succeed, you have to become really good at focusing on what you can control and then letting the rest take care of itself.

Every business, no matter what size it is or what industry it's in, has its share of complexity. Whether it's a multinational corporation or a local diner, there are a million different aspects to consider and keep track of. If you go looking for advice, you can find a million different advisors; from books and blogs to the actual people you pay to advise you. They will give you this suggestion, that admonition, and the other "secret sauce" for what you *have* to do to make your business work. It's incredibly easy to get lost in the weeds.

> Find what you can control and focus on that.

Forget about the complexity for a moment. As a leader, it's your job to get your head above the weeds, look around you, and see the big picture. If you don't, if you let yourself be led around by all that advice and all those details, you'll just break the teeth off all the gears that hold the whole thing up.

Don't get me wrong, it's important to get the details right. And you need to have the right people in place who know how to manage their areas, people you can trust to do it right so that you're running a tight ship. It's not your job to personally keep track of every nut, bolt, rope, and engine part on the ship.

Your job is to make sure the ship is heading in the right direction.

The "secret" to making *any* business work is to figure out where your leverage is, the point where you have some tangible influence, and then focus all your time, energy, effort, leadership, money, and everything else you've got on those things that will move your business forward.

The thing you're looking for is like the ship's rudder. There are two things about the rudder that make it important. The first is that it determines which way the ship goes. The second, equally important to the first, is that *you can control it*. You can't control the ocean. You can't control the weather, or the seasons, or the tides. You *can* control the rudder. When you're looking to figure out where to put your focus, remember those two things. What is the key factor or factors that a) determine what direction this thing is headed in, and b) are in your sphere of control?

Once you find that rudder, put your hand on it and keep it there.

As we left the nineties behind and opened the next chapter of our company's story, finding that rudder was Job One.

Set Your Ego Aside

When Rick and I stepped into the CEO's office, it was the first time in a decade that the company was being run by people who grew up within the company, rather than by someone brought in from the outside. It was an incredible opportunity, a chance for the two of us to seize this thing by the horns and shape it into the truly massive success we both knew in our hearts it had the potential to be. It was our chance to serve hundreds of our friends who worked at the company, and tens of thousands of loyal men and women in the field.

It was also one enormous challenge.

No matter how big the responsibilities or how broad the authority, it's an awful lot easier being number two than moving into the hot seat as number one. It's always easy to say, "Boy, if I were in charge, here's what I'd do. . . ." Then the day comes when you wake up and say, "Wait a minute—I *am* in charge!" People don't realize just how giant a step it is from being the guy just one rung down the ladder from the guy at the top to *being* the guy at the top. All of a sudden, it's all on you.

For any leader, the greatest challenges are never the circumstances, the economy, the marketplace, the management, or the employees. Real leaders know that the greatest challenges come from within themselves.

Leadership is like money. It doesn't change who you are or make you into a different person. It takes who and what you already were and amplifies that. Any issues you might have, whether it's with ego, insecurity, the ability to get along with others, or whatever else, are all on display when you step into the spotlight of leadership, and they're all brighter, bigger, and bolder than ever.

> Real leaders know that the greatest challenges come from within themselves.

The key here is awareness and self-knowledge. You have to be brutally honest with yourself. What are your weaknesses and potential pitfalls? The more honest you are, the more aware you are, the better positioned you are not to let this challenge get in the way.

For Rick and me, the first potential pitfall was *us*—and more specifically, the fact that there were two of us.

Typically, having two people share the CEO spot is a recipe for disaster. When you've got two CEOs, usually what happens is they end up fighting each other, each one trying to destroy the other to be the big honcho. Big ego is what ultimately spells the death of most businesses.

Fortunately for us, we'd already had years of working together in our "anchors to windward" role. Those years had given us the time and the opportunity to learn each other's areas of strength and weakness and how we each complemented the other. We already had that functional relationship down cold. We each had our distinct areas of responsibility. I didn't try to do Rick's job, and he didn't try to do mine. We each took care of those areas where our strengths lay, which couldn't have been more opposite. That worked out perfectly. Everything Rick worried about, I didn't have to worry about. And everything I worried about, he knew he didn't have to think about. Between the two of us, we worried about everything. We had also sorted out how our different temperaments worked together when it came to decision time.

> Big ego is what ultimately spells the death of most businesses.

Rick is extremely patient and methodical, where I'm a spur-of-the-moment, make-a-decision-now kind of guy. We laugh at how he buys a car versus how I buy a car. Rick will have a spreadsheet mapped out. He's looked at every model and every feature, every variable, and weighed them all carefully against each other, before he lays down his money and takes possession. Me, I'll step out for lunch and decide to go buy a car. Done. I force Rick to make a decision quicker than he wants to, and he forces me to slow down. Because of that constant give and take, we typically ended up making pretty good decisions together.

The way I describe our relationship: it's 1 + 1 = 11.

It wasn't as if we operated in isolation from each other. As I said, it's an organism, not an organization, and you can't completely separate marketing from operations, or sales from administration. We consulted with each other constantly, taking the other's perspective into account and using it to check-and-balance our own. We were both involved in every major decision. Rick never made major financial moves without the two of us sitting down and talking about it first. Likewise, I never launched any big marketing initiatives without talking it over first with Rick. We approached being co-CEOs as a very participatory process, but we each knew our own strengths and played to those strengths.

What really made Rick's and my relationship work, though, was that we never competed to see who was going to come out on top. Neither of us had our ego going up against the other. Yes, we had perfectly complementary skill sets. Rick takes care of the financial and operational side of things. I focused more on marketing strategy and leading the field. Having complimentary skills was important. What was far more important was that we both had the ability to take our own ego down a notch and not think we had to have the answer for everything.

What You Focus on Grows

Another potential pitfall, whenever you step into a leadership role, has to do with the challenge of *succession*.

This is a big one. Taking over the reins from someone else always offers a huge opportunity to set a new course for the organization, along with the equally huge temptation to bad-mouth the previous leadership. When new CEOs take over, often the very first thing they do is tell everyone how terrible the person who came before them was and make a big deal out of all the problems that person left behind. That buys them some time and maybe some good will. I've noticed that politicians tend to do this too, always blaming their biggest problems on the previous administration.

Here's the problem: If you do that, you're focusing your people on the negative. You may think that talking down your predecessor gives you the chance to look good by comparison, but if you do, you're kidding yourself. Human nature doesn't work that way. Once you start focusing people on the negative, the negative is what they start seeing. And what people see is what they'll tend to do.

Here's the good news about human nature: Whatever you focus on, that's what you get more of. Here's the bad news about human nature: Whatever you focus on, that's what you get more of!

If you're coaching a kid on a baseball team who's up at the plate, what do you tell that kid?

You can say, "Now, Billy, whatever you do, don't strike out! Don't mess up, buddy, your whole team's counting on you, so no matter what, do not swing and miss!" Keep doing that, and Billy doesn't have a chance. You and I both know what's going to happen. The poor kid is going to strike out. You've hammered it into him so hard, now he can't think about anything *but* striking out.

> Once you start focusing people on the negative, the negative is what they start seeing.

That's not how to coach effectively. Here's what you want to say: "Okay, Billy, you got this, buddy. Just keep your cool, stay loose and ready, and keep your eye on that ball. If it looks bad, let it go. But if it looks good to you, you show it what you're made of and knock it out of here. Don't worry about the team, don't worry about the score, they'll take care of themselves. Right now it's just you and that ball, nothing else—just you and that ball."

Focus Billy on hitting the ball, and you've just boosted the odds of him hitting it out of the park.

What you focus on is what you get. In fact, what you focus on grows.

If you focus on your problems, they're going to grow. If you focus on what's wrong, more things keep going wrong. As a leader, if you spend time criticizing the way your predecessor screwed things up, all you're doing is inviting criticism to flourish. Pretty soon you'll be the one it's directed at.

A house built on a bed of criticism is doomed. Put energy into blaming your predecessor, and sooner or later people will realize that all you're doing is evading responsibility.

Fortunately for Rick and me, this challenge—like the challenge of having two CEOs—was no challenge at all. We had talked this issue over thoroughly, long before Joe left and we became co-CEOs. We were in complete agreement about it. We emphatically did *not* want to negate or in any way run down the leadership that had come before. We'd both seen it happen a hundred times, a thousand times. It's always poison. Right within our own Primerica culture, we'd already seen firsthand how detrimental it could be to have people stuck in the past.

Besides, it just wasn't our style. Both by design and by our natures, we were determined we were never going to say anything bad about anybody that came before us. And we never did. We had already been through a ton of cultural changes at the company. We didn't want to try to change the culture. We wanted to honor it but take it further. We wanted to take the best of what made A.L. Williams great in the eighties, and the best of what Joe and Pete and the others had brought to the table in the nineties, and focus it all on explosive growth in the new century.

Respect the past. Live in the present. Focus on the future.

Figure Out What You Can Control

We knew how to work together. We knew we needed to focus on moving forward without denigrating the past. The $64,000 question—or in Primerica's case, more like the $6.4 billion question—was, again: focus on *what* exactly?

What was our growth strategy?

During the nineties, the executive leadership had tried all kinds of strategies to stimulate more growth. Often these strategies were aimed either at those people in our sales force who weren't producing much, to get them to do more; or at people who'd quit the sales force in the past, to get them to come back. A lot of energy and effort went into trying to figure out what we could best do to get the "inactives" active again. As Rick and I took the helm in 2000, I was pretty sure I knew the answer to that question. I knew exactly what we could do to get all those people who'd quit over the years to come back. It came down to one word: *Nothing.*

> A big part of focusing on what you can control is *not* focusing on what you *can't.*

There was absolutely nothing we could do that would cause inactive people to suddenly become active again. When executives would ask, "What if we did this, or did that, or made this change or that change, could we get all those people who've quit to join us again?" The simple answer was: Nope. So let's not put energy into something we can't accomplish.

A big part of focusing on what you can control is *not* focusing on what you *can't.* Sounds simple, right? Yet it's amazing how much time, energy, and emotion people devote to focusing on things that are completely beyond their control.

We all do this, to some degree. It's human nature. I love the University of Georgia football team. I'm a big Bulldogs' fan and go to every game I can. Like a lot of sports fans, I have some peculiar habits in relation to my team. For example, I'll wear the same socks to every game, the same shirt, the same hat. If they get behind, I'll stand up and move to a different place. If they start winning, I'll stand right there in that exact spot for the rest of the game.

Why do I do these things? Out of the completely irrational sense that anything I do could have the slightest influence on the outcome of the game. Of course, that's just plain silly. The reality is that I have no control whatsoever over the next play or any player's behavior. I know that. There's a portion of my brain that fully understands that Georgia did not lose the game today because I couldn't find my lucky socks this morning. That's nothing but pure superstitious nonsense—and I do it anyway, laughing at myself as I do.

But not when it comes to business.

When it comes to the things that really matter, there's no room for indulgence or superstition. When it comes to business, I pay very close attention to what I can control and what I can't.

I cannot control Congress or the state of the economy. The president of the United States has so far not called me up and said, "Hey, John, what do you think we should do about this?" Neither has the chairman of the Federal Reserve. The reality is that I don't have any more influence on the state of the overall business climate than I do on the outcome of that Georgia ballgame.

What I have control over is what I do and how I behave every day.

"[I]n our world," wrote Tolstoy, "everybody thinks of changing humanity, and nobody thinks of changing himself." Whatever change you want to see in others, you have to *be* that change. If you want people to be more excited, then *you've* got to be more excited. If you want people to work harder, then *you've* got to work harder.

If more people spent more time working on themselves and less time complaining about everyone else, it'd be a much better world. People would be able to accomplish

> If you want people to work harder, then *you've* got to work harder.

a lot more. I'm not preaching morality here. This is simple physics. There are things you can influence and things you can't. Why waste time and energy on the latter?

People tend to be attracted to their distractions, but distractions are just places where you've got *no traction*. Because businesses are nothing but collections of people, businesses do the same thing. So many businesses pour enormous amounts of time and effort into trying to change things that will never change. You can push against the mountain all you want, but that doesn't mean the mountain's going to step aside.

So, back to the strategic question we faced in 2000: How do we increase the percentage of people in our sales force who are doing a significant amount of business? We could spend the next decade trying to come up with solutions to that puzzle, or we could just cut to the chase and accept the commonsense answer: *We don't.*

You could take all these thousands of people who haven't done anything in years and send them an inspiring letter about all the changes you're making and all the great things you're doing and how exciting this is gonna be. Will they suddenly start getting engaged? No, they won't. Sure, at the margins you can improve people's productivity, but by and large, when someone's done, they're done. Throwing alarm clocks into the cemetery won't raise the dead, and planting a dead stick in the ground doesn't make it a tree. You can plant it, water it, and fertilize it all you want. It's not going to grow.

You can't change human nature. You can't force people to be what they're not or do what they don't want to do. People are people. They're going to do what they're going to do. You can't change their buying habits. You can't change their preferences.

Apple became the largest technology company in the world by building devices people could use the way they wanted to, instead of trying to make people adapt themselves to how the devices wanted to be used, which is what everyone else was doing. Southwest Airlines became the number one carrier in the United States by letting people fly the way they wanted to—no penalties for changing flights, no penalties for booking flights one leg at a time, no extra charges for luggage—instead of trying to force their customers to accept the way the airline wanted them to do it like everyone else was doing.

These companies became incredibly successful by facing the realities they were dealing with, and working with them instead of trying to change them. They focused on what they could control, and didn't try to affect what they could not control.

The reality we were facing in our business was that it's a volunteer army. In our business, we attract part-time people. They're going to do what they're going to do. We don't get to decide who joins. And we're always going to attract a lot of people who join just because they like to join things. There are plenty of people who will join anything. They'll go to the meetings, and they'll have a great time being part of the excitement. They love the feeling of belonging to something. The majority of them aren't necessarily going to really *do* anything major. We'll never change that.

What we needed weren't more joiners. What we needed were leaders. A lot of people start out as joiners, maybe without even realizing they have leadership in them, and develop into leaders only once they're in the right environment with the right support. But you can't tell who's who when they first join. You have to just let them be who they are. The only way we were going to get more leaders was to bring in a *lot* more people and let the leaders show up, like cream rising to the top. The reality of our business is that you have to attract a ton of joiners to find a handful of leaders. That's just the way it is.

We didn't need our people to do more. We just needed more people.

And there was our answer. Our growth strategy starting in 2000 boiled down to three words: *Focus on recruiting.*

Our corporate leaders throughout the nineties had viewed recruiting as one *part* of the whole equation, but that wasn't going to do it. It had to be *the most important part* of the equation. Recruiting had to be the tip of the spear. Without that sharp point, all we'd have was a big stick.

To explain the strategy to our team in Duluth, I told them about the car I had had back when I was a college freshman, a red 1973 Ford Maverick. That car had terrible alignment, and there wasn't one darn thing you could do about it. You could leave it at the best shop in town and get it adjusted absolutely spot-on perfect, and when that thing hit a bump in the road five minutes after you picked it up, *Blam!* There it went, right back out of alignment again.

This, as I explained to my team, was a condition that was *beyond my control.*

Pretty soon I figured out what I had to do. If I wanted to make that thing go straight, I had to oversteer it to the left. It was that simple. I had to accept the condition I couldn't control, and compensate for it.

"This business is just like my red '73 Maverick," I told the team. "The thing that drives our field is human nature. People have problems in their lives. They have challenges. They quit. We can't stop that. We can't make them *not* quit, and when they do, we can't make them come back. There's not one thing in the world we can do about it. That's how they're aligned. If we want this company to grow, we have to oversteer it toward recruiting. We have to focus everything we do on supporting the field to recruit. The message has got to be consistently *recruiting.*"

That was our rudder.

The thing that made our business work was pretty simple: new people bringing in new people. If we didn't have that happening, we weren't growing. And if we weren't growing, then we were dying.

You're either green and growing, or you're ripe and rotten.

This business is all about momentum. The thing is always in motion, at all times either growing or declining. It never stays put like a constant number. Any time you take your foot off the gas and try to coast, Murphy's Law tends to take over and make hash out of things. Momentum is a lot easier to lose than it is to build, and when you lose it, you better fight like a junkyard dog to get it back.

> You're either green and growing, or you're ripe and rotten.

This was exactly what we had to do now.

Condition People for Success

Leaving home for college in the fall of 1975 was one of the toughest transitions of my life. Looking back it seems almost ludicrous to me now. The University of Georgia in Athens was barely fifty miles away from where my parents and I lived, less than an hour's drive. Obviously I could come home at anytime to visit. But to me, I might as well have been heading off to the University of Alaska. I was leaving my home, my friends, my neighborhood, and going off to live in a strange environment with thousands of students and gigantic classes.

Arriving at the campus in Athens was an experience of total culture shock. I'd grown up in a tiny community on the outskirts of a town of maybe five thousand people. Now there were four times that many people just in my *school*.

One of my first classes, Political Science 101, took place in a huge amphitheater with several hundred students. I took a seat in the back row and looked around. A lot of these students had come from the wealthier sections of Atlanta and gone to prep schools. They were ready for this place and looked like they fit right in. I felt like I'd relocated to Mars.

That first day of class, the girl sitting in front of me raised her hand. When the professor called on her she said, "Are we going to receive a syllabus today?"

A *syllabus*? What on earth was that? I had not the slightest clue what the word meant. I thought, *The class hasn't even started yet, and I'm already behind!* Had these people all taken a course in how to go to college? Because they all seemed like they knew what was going on, what to expect, what to do, and I was absolutely lost.

After that demoralizing political science class, I went back to my dorm room and called my dad from a pay phone at the end of the hall. "Dad," I said. "I hate it here. I don't like the people. I don't like the place, and I don't want to stay. I don't know what I'm doing here. I want to quit school, come home, and get a job."

He said, "Look, Son. We've already paid your tuition. You're already there. Tell you what. Wait till Christmas, and then we'll make a decision."

"Okay," I said. "I'll give it a shot." I hung up feeling heavyhearted. Christmas seemed like an awful long way away.

That first semester at college was the first and only time in my life when I found myself saying, "Okay, so *this* is what being depressed is all about."

A few weeks later, we had our first political science exam. When they handed around our graded papers, I was thrilled to see I'd made a 98. I peeked over at the girl who sat in front of me, the one who'd asked about the syllabus on day one. Because of the slope in the amphitheater seating, if I leaned forward a little I could just see her paper as she looked at it.

She'd gotten a 46.

I sat back in my seat, stunned, the realization echoing around my brain like a thunderclap. This girl had almost made me quit! Of course, she didn't know that. And it wasn't actually her who had almost made me quit. The fact was that I'd been just looking for a reason to disqualify myself, a reason to say "I'm not good enough." It was *me* who almost made *me* quit.

Now, this was weird. It wasn't like I'd grown up with parents who told me I was a loser. I didn't come from a miserable home. I had two of the greatest parents anyone could wish for. They never yelled at me, never hit me, always encouraged me and believed in me. I had a very happy childhood. Yet here I was, fully expecting myself to fail, for absolutely no good reason. I had this deep sense of inadequacy, this conviction that I wasn't good enough. Where did *that* come from?

I'm now convinced that it just comes with the territory. It's part of being a human being in the world. People are designed for success but get conditioned for failure.

You are not supposed to be broke. You are not designed to settle for mediocrity. But somewhere along the line, the world starts beating you down, programming you with the idea that life is hard. It starts telling you that as soon as you get out of school you're going to go "get a job," which is code for "go find something that'll allow you to just get by." Day-by-day, week-by-week, you gradually give up on your dreams and start accepting what you think life has to offer.

Of course, if you had an espe-cially tough time as a child, growing up with people who were constantly cutting you down and undermining your confidence, then it's easy to understand how you'd arrive at adulthood carrying a pretty big burden of belief that you were a failure. But what I was seeing in myself shocked me. I

> People are designed for success but get conditioned for failure.

realized that it doesn't take a terrible, abusive, Charles Dickens type of childhood to do that to you. Because even if you grow up in the most supportive environment imaginable, it seems to be part of our human nature that we beat up on ourselves. Yes, circumstances can put up roadblocks and smash potholes in our path. But far more insidious are the ways we undermine our own forward motion ourselves.

They say most plane crashes happen in the first 90 seconds after take-off. I think most careers are like that too. We sabotage ourselves and talk ourselves into outright failure or its sullen cousin, mediocrity, before we've even gotten started. Right there in my first week of college, I'd almost quit school. I've often wondered: if I had quit, how differently might my life have gone?

Most people wake up every day looking for a reason not to win, a reason not to do great things in their lives. Looking for a reason to fail. Some people, as the saying goes, never miss an opportunity to miss an opportunity. When they see a doorway of great possibility open in front of them, they turn the other way.

I've seen people who started out in life with an "I'm gonna conquer the world" mindset. As the years tick by, that optimism fades. They start living in the past. By the time they're 20, they're already reminiscing about the high school football days. By 25, all they talk about is what they did in college. Some people are old at 30; the best of their life is behind them. Yet I've met 80-year-olds who are incredibly young. Chronological age is completely beside the point. I don't care how old you are, if you want to live your best life, if you want to be someone who leads others, who makes a difference in the world, then you need to be focused on the incredible possibilities that lie ahead on the path at your feet.

I believe the single most important factor in your success is to take responsibility for where you are in your life and for moving forward from there. You're the one who sits where you sit, the one whose task it is to figure out what you need to do now to get to someplace better.

You will never rise above the image you have of yourself. And the person in charge of that image is *you*. Nobody else. You are in charge of your life—not the people who doubt you, not the people who question you, not the people who put you down, not the people who look down their noses at you. If you want to win, don't waste any time beating yourself up about the mistakes you've made or the ways you think you don't measure up. You can't let life overwhelm you. You have to be the one who goes out there and overwhelms life, the one who seizes life by the horns and wrestles it to the ground.

Taking responsibility for your life doesn't guarantee you're going to do well, or that you're going to succeed. In fact, it doesn't guarantee much. But it does guarantee this: that whatever happens, you're the one behind your own steering wheel.

I don't know if I can say this came to me as a fully formed revelation, exactly, sitting there in my

> You will never rise above the image you have of yourself.

freshman political science class, and I wouldn't say I exactly went out there and *overwhelmed life*. But I did finish that first semester with pretty decent grades. I started to have a glimmer of understanding that I was the person in charge of my life. That in order to be a winner, I would have to start looking at myself as a winner, talking like a winner, acting like a winner, thinking like a winner.

This was how the whole team at Primerica needed to start thinking again. During the nineties, we had experienced a period of changing visions for the company. The company had made a lot of positive strides, but all the changes had also taken a toll.

On the positive side of the ledger, we focused on needs-based selling and implemented business systems that allowed the company to navigate a changing regulatory environment. But these changes also had our team wrestling with how to build their businesses. I felt that we were applying the gas pedal and the brakes at the same time.

The changes were very important—critical in the IPO process a decade later—but our sales force was more focused on what and how to do business and not on *why* to do the business. They and we were focused on the business as a business and not a cause. We wanted to keep all the good that had been done and unleash the fun and excitement in the business.

Light a Fire *Within* People, Not *Under* Them

Rick and I knew what our growth strategy was: Focus on recruiting. The next question was: How exactly were we going to put that into action? We could *talk* about recruiting till we were blue in the face, but we couldn't force anyone to go out and do it. *They* were the ones who had to go out and do it. "They," in this case, meant about 80,000 independent agents spread throughout the country. People who were not on the payroll. People who were 100 percent volunteers and didn't *have* to do anything.

A lot of people in the sales business talk about training and business systems. An enormous amount of time, energy, and money goes into devising new ways of training people how to do the business. But it's not about the training. It's not about the system. And it's not about the thousand and one ways the products are great or all the product information you can cram into a website. You can take the same great products, the same brilliant system, the same time-tested training, and still wind up with thousands of people at a dead standstill because people are not going to care much about the *how* or the *what* until they are first inspired, motivated, and plugged in to their *why*.

Too often leaders think they can get results by lighting a fire under people. That rarely works. When it does work, it doesn't last for long. If you want real results, you have to light a fire *within* people. Instead of trying to focus them on what you want them to do; you have to focus them on why they want to do it.

Bottom line: Primerica is not at its core an insurance business, or even a financial services business. At its core, it's a *people* business.

In fact, this is true for any business. Every business is a people business, and people are pretty much the same wherever you go. People are people are people. They want to be made to feel special. They want to be recognized. Before they're going to be interested in focusing on all the details and particulars of their job or task, they want to be part of something exciting, something fun, something compelling, something *great*. Every organization is ultimately driven by a sense of mission and the importance of what the people in it are accomplishing. If it isn't, then people are just punching a clock, and that won't take anyone very far. Simply doing it, whatever the "it" is, to earn a paycheck is just not going to cut it for long.

> Instead of trying to focus them on what you want them to do; you have to focus them on why they want to do it.

Logic would tell you that the people in our sales force are here for the money, right? After all, there's a pretty significant financial opportunity here. Some of our people, those who've been here for years and grown tremendously in their leadership abilities, have been able to build up to some truly impressive income levels (as we'll see a little later on). Boe Adams, one of the company's legendary figures going back to the early days of A.L. Williams, used to say, "For salespeople, the most sensitive nerve in the body runs from the wallet to the brain." Boe had a good point. As I said, the key indicator that corporate always needs to have their eye on is *checks to the field*.

But what I'd learned through my years with the company was that even though they do it for the money, *they don't do it for the money*. Is that a contradiction? Yes, it is. It's also true.

> Every organization is ultimately driven by a sense of mission and the importance of what the people in it are accomplishing.

Is the money important? Of course. But by itself, the money's not enough. You can have all kinds of financial incentives in place, but if you have a toxic environment with terrible communication, no recognition, and no sense of adventure or fun, then all the financial incentives in the world aren't going to get that thing off the ground.

People are people. Yes, they need to run their households, and obviously, the money has to work or it isn't worth their time. The money may even have been the driving reason they looked at joining Primerica in the first place. Hey, if you stuck a microphone in their face and asked them, "Why are you here? Why are you in this business?" they might even *tell* you that it's to make extra household income, to provide for their families, to help make ends meet. But I can promise you, *the money is secondary*. That's not what makes them stick, and it's not what makes them grow.

What makes them stick, what makes them grow, is *how they feel about what they're doing*. When things aren't going well, when things are a struggle, *that's* what keeps them going.

And bottom line, *that* was the biggest problem we faced as Rick and I took office. Little by little, we had been drifting away from this simple truth for years.

Our meetings had become too focused on things, content, the how-to. New products, new presentations, new tactics and new ways of conducting the business. Don't get me wrong. Knowing your product inside and out, being properly trained in how to talk to people, having the knowledge that drives your business, these are all important. But that wasn't our problem. We had that part down. The information was all good, but effective meetings aren't about information. A meeting isn't just a meeting. It's an *event*.

An event can't just be a product symposium, where everybody walks out the door with their heads filled up with product knowledge. If you want to light fires *within* people, you have to create something that inspires people to go home and start calling, e-mailing, and texting their friends to say, "Wow, you have *got* to be here at the next one!" Your event has to become a showcase of success.

Over time, our focus had become business, business, business. I wanted to get us back to people, people, people—the spirit of the family, the team, who we are, our cause and our mission. I wanted to get us back to the understanding that this wasn't just a great business, but that we were changing people's lives.

We couldn't control what the sales force did. We couldn't control what *anyone* did, except ourselves. What we could control was what kind of message we gave out from the home office and where we focused people's attention. That was pretty much it. That's what we had to work with. Everything else would be a waste of energy.

What you focus on grows. If we created an environment of fun and excitement and a sense of shared mission, focused everything within that environment on recruiting, then recruiting would grow.

At least, that was the idea. Would it work? We'd soon find out.

Put the Fun Back in Fundamentals

We had to hit the ground running, so we didn't waste any time.

We wanted to take all the good that had been accomplished and jump-start recruiting. You can't wait for success to create an environment of excitement. That's backwards. You have to create excitement first because you need excitement in order to generate success. We had to *show* them that things were going to be different. We had to create something exciting, something that would have everyone talking. And that's exactly what we did.

In January 2000, we held a meeting in Atlanta with about 500 of our national sales director teams to kick off the new era. Our theme was One Team, One Dream. This wasn't about Rick and John, and it wasn't about the corporate team over here and the sales force over there. It was about us—the Big Us. The collective team.

"We're going to do great things together," we told our leaders. "While most companies focus on earnings per share, we're going to be focused on earnings per *chair*."

That January meeting turned into something more like a revival meeting than a company conference. The level of spirit and enthusiasm in that room was electric. The five-hundred-odd people who were there took the spirit of that day out to the rest of the field, and people started getting lit up again everywhere.

During that meeting, we also kept coming back to this core message:

"We're going to put the fun back in fundamentals."

Our number one task that year was to make the entire environment at Primerica more fun. We had to get back to having fun, without repudiating all the compliance elements that had been put in place to make the business work better. That became our rallying cry for the rest of that year.

And it wasn't just talk. We instituted new programs to drive the message home.

This being 2000, we created something called the Millennium Leaders Council, which was essentially an incentive program for brand new reps. Every month, based on their numbers in recruiting new people and sales production for their first 100 days in the business, people could qualify to be part of the Council. We would fly the top 100 to Atlanta every month to be in the audience and be recognized in my monthly TV broadcast. We would chauffeur them in from the airport, and when they got to headquarters we had a red carpet out there for them. We treated them like royalty, because they *were* royalty. New people were the lifeblood of the business, and we acted like it.

We put a tremendous amount of emphasis on field incentives. Not just incentives to earn cash bonuses, but incentives to earn cash plus all kinds of recognition. We expanded our contests and dramatically increased the number of slots people could win. We designed it so that more people *at all levels* of the sales force could win, not just the folks toward the top of the company. We made it so that more new people could win, and made recruiting a more important part of our contests.

Things began to grow. And grow. And then they grew some more.

Over the months after that first leadership event we started seeing significant momentum, both in recruiting and in sales. That momentum lasted throughout that year and kept right on going.

Be Clear on Your Purpose

One day in the early fall of the following year, I was in Washington, DC, at a board meeting of the Direct Selling Association. The DSA has represented direct selling companies for more than a hundred years. During the nineties, we had worked with some people from their organization and bit-by-bit developed a strong association with them. They're great people, and it's a great organization. At this point I was serving on the board of directors.

On this particular Tuesday, while I was in an early morning meeting there, I got a phone call from Dayna, my long-time executive assistant, who told me I needed to tune to the news. We switched on the TV in the boardroom and saw the World Trade Center in flames.

A few minutes later the second plane hit.

We were meeting at the St. Regis hotel, a few blocks down from the White House. Just outside our doors the military was already heading up the street. It was chaos out there. Some of my colleagues were saying they thought they might have to make arrangements to catch a flight out of DC that afternoon.

"I don't think so, guys," I said. "This is a whole different thing." I knew right away that all air traffic was going to be grounded, and not just for a few hours.

I got on the phone with my office and was able to get a ride through one of our senior national sales directors from North Carolina, Andy Young, who is one of my best friends on the face of the planet. Andy has family, as well as a large organization, in the DC area, and he got me set up right away. Andy's brother Randy and his sister Debbie drove me and my friend Stuart Johnson down to Greensboro, where Andy met us and drove us the rest of the way down to Georgia.

When I reached the office, plans were already under way for a special event we would hold a few weeks later in the New York metro area as a tribute to the people who had perished in the attacks. Our sales force was very strong in the New York and New Jersey area, so it had a huge personal impact on many of our field leaders, who had lost close friends there.

The events of September 11 were both tragic and sobering for everyone in the country. For us at Primerica, they also had the effect of shedding a stark light on the reason we were all there, doing what we were doing. Every time there's a major tragedy where many people die, it always brings into clear focus the importance of what we do because it directly affects our clients. We are, after all, first and foremost a life insurance company. Helping families cope with the impact of loss is what we do. The reason Art founded this company was to make sure ordinary Americans were as fully protected from financial catastrophe as possible.

Let me give you just one example.

We had a brand new agent in New York at the time who went out and created her first client on Sunday, September 9, a man named Miguel Alvarez.

Miguel was a classic American success story. An immigrant from the Dominican Republic, Miguel had a lovely wife and three daughters. He also had a fantastic job as maître d' at Windows on the World, one of the most famous restaurants in New York City. (Note: I'm using pseudonyms here to protect the family's privacy.)

Miguel wanted to get the policy, but his wife was reluctant. She saw it as one more bill they'd have to pay every month. The agent was very encouraging and pointed out that the family had no insurance and no savings, not a nickel, other than what Miguel earned at his job. Between Miguel and the agent, they convinced Mrs. Alvarez to let them go ahead and write the policy. The agent wrote the application right away, that Sunday, and planned to turn it in to the local Primerica office a few days later, on Tuesday evening. That is, on the evening of September 11.

As maître d', Miguel would not normally have been at the restaurant at eight o'clock in the morning. But for whatever reason, on that particular Tuesday he went in early. Windows on the World was situated at the top of the North Tower. He was there when the plane hit.

We didn't actually have Miguel's application in our office at the time (in the chaos of the day's events, the agent wasn't able to turn it in as planned), so strictly speaking the policy was not yet in effect. It didn't matter to us. They say "Intent is nine-tenths of the law." The Alvarezes' intent was good enough for us. We paid the claim in full, immediately, and gave our rep a check to deliver to the family for $250,250.

"I cannot imagine what would have happened to that family with three daughters and zero income, if they hadn't taken out that policy. It really drove home to me what it is we do at Primerica," Joan White, the agent who delivered the check to Mrs. Alvarez, later related.

We had clients on every plane, in every building. We paid $10 million in death claims in connection with September 11.

A few weeks later, we put on our event at the Meadowlands in New Jersey. The whole purpose of the event was to pay tribute to the people who had died and express support for their families. It also served to underline the seriousness and importance of what we do for our clients. It ended up having the effect of further focusing our entire sales force.

Yes, building financial success was important. Yes, having a lot of fun while doing it was equally important. But more than anything, we were all here together to help as many people as we possibly could to make their lives better—both in the good times and the bad.

Boom Times

Back in March 2000, just a few months after Rick and I took over the CEO spot, the Nasdaq crashed, the dot-com bubble burst, and the overall business climate began to darken. Now, in the months after 9/11, the whole economy slid into the pits, as a full decade of record economic growth began grinding to a halt. But not at Primerica. The souring economy didn't especially touch us. In 2002 and beyond, our business continued to grow.

When Rick and I took over at the end of 1999, Primerica had about 79,000 licensed life insurance reps in the field. By the end of 2006, we were over 100,000 strong. During that time, sales force cash flow went from a little over $400 million annually to over $600 million annually.

One of our goals was to significantly increase the number of people earning six figures. When you're earning $100,000 or more per year, you're bringing in more than $8,000 a month. In my experience, most families can run their household on that without feeling a pinch. That's full-time income.

When you increase the number of six-figure earners, you also automatically increase the number of seven-figure earners, that elite group of people who are earning a million or more a year. That's important, too, because even though these folks are by definition always going to be a tiny minority, they also serve as a very real inspiration to the rest of the field. And that's not all. When you increase your number of six-figure earners, that also means you're increasing the number of five-figure earners—the part-timers who are bringing in $800 to a few thousand dollars a month. For these folks, that can mean a car payment, a house payment, or even the difference between making it versus going under. These guys and gals are in many ways the heart and soul of the business.

From 2000 to 2006 the company *doubled* the number of $100,000 earners and doubled the number of million-dollar earners.

These years were amazing. In the summer of 2001, we held our biennial convention in the Georgia Dome, an enormous

FIGURE 5.1 **Cash Flow to the Sales Force, 1999–2007**

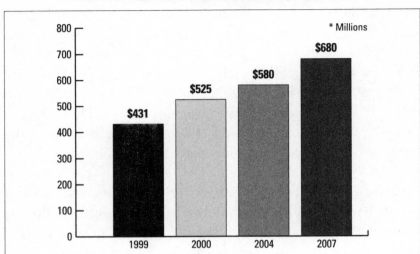

stadium in the heart of downtown Atlanta. We did the same in 2003, 2005, and 2007. For both the 2001 and 2003 conventions, I hired a motor coach to drive out to Salem and pick up my Mom and all her friends—including my uncle, A.W. Dalton—and ferry them over to the Dome in Atlanta, where they were seated in VIP seats down in front. They got to see Little Johnny up there in front, talking to those thousands of cheering Primericans.

I'll never forget the look on my mom's face that night in Atlanta. I'd made her proud. No better feeling in the world.

Business had never been better. By the mid-2000s, we were receiving so much mail that the U.S. Postal Service gave us our own zip code.

We were on a roll. There was no stopping us.

At least, that's how it seemed at the time.

PRACTICE #5

Focus on What You Can Control

As the leader, you have to be the most focused person on the team. There are some things you can control and some you can't. The secret to making *any* business work is to figure out where you have the most tangible influence and then focus everything on those things that will move your business forward. What you focus on grows.

* A real leader knows that the greatest challenges come from within. Be brutally honest with yourself. Ask yourself: what are my weaknesses and potential pitfalls? The more aware you are, the better positioned you are not to let this challenge get in the way.

* Treat your predecessors with respect and give them the benefit of the doubt. It can be tempting to badmouth the leadership that came before you, but doing so will only weaken your own leadership. Focus on what you need to do, not what your predecessors did. Take the best of what came before, and focus on what you need to do to build for the future.

* You can't change human nature. You can't change your customers, your employees, or anyone else. All you can change is what *you* do. There are things you can influence and things you can't. Why waste time and energy on the latter?

* You won't get real results trying to light a fire under people. You need to light a fire within them. Rather than trying to focus them on *what* you want them to do, focus them on *why* they want to do it. A manager tells people what to do. A leader helps people find why they're doing it.

ACTION STEP

In your present situation—business, organization, career—list those factors influencing growth that you *can* control, and those you *can't*. Among those you can, choose which one you think is most important. In other words: *Find your rudder.*

CHAPTER 6

Mortality

Develop a Peaceful Core

> A peaceful mind generates power.
>
> —NORMAN VINCENT PEALE

One of my father's favorite authors was a turn-of-the-century Massachusetts writer named David Grayson. Actually, that was his pen name. When he wasn't escaping into the peace and quiet of his pseudonym, "Grayson" was a famous journalist named Ray Stannard Baker.

Back in the early 1900s, Stannard Baker was a very important man, a newspaper reporter for the extremely influential *McClure's* magazine and one of a group of writers, known as the "muckrakers," who took on crooked politicians and industry barons. At the end of World War I, he served as Woodrow Wilson's press secretary at the peace negotiations at Versailles. His was a colorful, high-flying career, and it took its toll.

Baker eventually got burned out living in the political fast lane and reached the point where he nearly had a nervous breakdown. Instead, he had a breakthrough. He discovered one of the greatest leadership secrets there is: the value of developing a peaceful core.

Find Your Peaceful Core

After deciding it was time to quit the big-city rat race, Baker bought a farm in the bucolic Massachusetts college town of Amherst and started writing about the country and simple living. His David Grayson books, including *Adventures in Contentment*, *Adventures in Solitude*, and *Under My Elm*, sold more than two million copies. For those days, those were James Patterson numbers. Grayson's home has been turned into a fraternity house and is on the walking tour of Amherst College. The elm tree he used to sit under to think, ponder, and write still stands there. They call it the Grayson Elm.

Grayson wrote about the importance of developing a peaceful core. Following that wisdom has been crucial to maintaining sanity throughout my life.

Human beings mess up. Regardless of your particular philosophy or beliefs, that is one basic fact of life you can't really argue. There's just way too much empirical evidence. We try, and we do some great things, but no matter who we are, inevitably we do stupid stuff. So does everyone else.

The world is always going to be a messed up place. You're going to have calamities and chaos and crises and catastrophes. All kinds of things will go wrong. It's just the way the world is. You can't control that. But you *can* control whether or not there's chaos on the inside.

If you let that outer chaos seep into your mind and heart, if you have a storm of struggle and confusion whipping around in your inner self, then hoping to be effective in the outer world is going to be a losing battle. To achieve anything of substance, you've got to reach a point where you carry a sense of peace at your center, regardless of whatever craziness is going on around you. Otherwise it will all drive *you* crazy.

In his classic, *The Power of Positive Thinking*, Norman Vincent Peale titled one of his chapters, "A Peaceful Mind Generates Power." I believe that's one of the greatest leadership secrets anyone's ever been able to pinpoint.

A sense of inner peace acts like the gyroscope in an aircraft that enables it to adjust its flight path and stay on course. The only way you can make it through all the chaos intact is by having a peaceful core, a place inside of you that is content in who you are with all your best intentions and all your imperfections. If you reach that point of peace, then you can weather the storms.

> To achieve anything of substance, you've got to reach a point where you carry a sense of peace at your center.

Many people develop this peaceful core through their faith and religious practice. Some read the Bible or other inspirational readings every day. Some people swear by meditation, or practice martial arts. One way I do it is by spending time in the country.

Over my years in business, I've put in a lot of time on the golf course, relaxing with associates and sometimes talking over some critical issue or other between greens. But to be honest, golf is not my idea of recreation. I'd much rather spend the day digging in the dirt, planting trees, working on my garden. Even at the most hectic times in my career, I'd spend all weekend every chance I got messing around on my little farm. Right now, as these words hit the paper, I've got a big raised-bed garden with 43 tomato plants I'll be putting in tomorrow. There is nothing I love as much as getting in my truck, going to the nursery, buying up a ton of plants, and filling the back bed with them, then coming back and spending the day digging and planting. It's the one thing I can do where I'm not worried about anything else or even *thinking* about anything else.

Not long ago, I had the chance to talk with Winston Churchill's great-grandson, Duncan Sandys (pronounced "sands"), who lives in Atlanta. Duncan told me that when he was going through all his great-grandfather's papers, he couldn't help noticing how much the man talked about painting. Churchill was an accomplished painter who produced more than 500 works. (One of his most famous, "The Tower of the Katoubia Mosque," he painted as a gift to Franklin Roosevelt during World War II.) The remarkable thing is that Churchill never took a single formal lesson and never held a brush in his hand until the age of 40.

Duncan said his great-grandfather talked a good deal about how, when he was going through times of trial and struggle, the thing that most kept him at peace was his painting. Standing in front of a blank canvas and creating with oils was Churchill's way of finding that peaceful core.

"If it weren't for painting," he wrote in his book *Painting as a Pastime*, "I could not live, I could not bear the strain of things."

I know just how he felt. That's how I feel about digging in the dirt.

As a leader, sometimes you deal with the challenges and issues that other people caused, problems that aren't your fault and that you had nothing to do with creating. As a leader, that's your job description: dealing with stuff you didn't cause but needs fixing anyway. And sometimes you're dealing with the fallout from stupid things you did yourself. Happens to all of us.

But that's okay because a peaceful core generates the power to deal with all that.

Knowing and practicing this has been a crucial force in my life. It has allowed me to stay sane and calm, especially during times of stress. The greater the stress, the more I depended on returning to that peaceful core.

Little did I know, in the early months of 2006, that my life would depend on it.

A Dark Moment

When Loveanne and I woke up on the beautiful island of Oahu, on the morning of February 12, 2006, neither of us had the slightest idea that an event was about to occur that would affect the course of our lives.

We were there in Hawaii, hardly a place you'd think of as one of foreboding or danger, as part of a trip celebrating the incredible achievements of our sales force, soon to be joined by hundreds of Primerica reps who had won their place in the celebration.

The business was absolutely flying, and these incentive trips were a critical part of it. As I said, people will do more for recognition, for fun, or for a sense of being part of something big than they will purely for money. The previous year, we'd held a huge event in Orlando, where we rented out not one but two hotels-—the Ritz-Carlton and the JW Marriott. We took over the entire Universal Studios for one night for our exclusive use. (For that night, as I told the crowd, it wasn't Universal Studios— it was Primerica Studios.) But this Hawaii trip was our biggest yet. All through the second half of 2005, people had worked extremely hard to grow their businesses and hit the targets that would qualify them to join us in Oahu, and a record-setting number of them had done it. About 1,500 couples were coming to spend a few days with us, so many people that we'd had to split it into two phases. The first phase had just ended, and the next group was coming in the following day, February 13, to start our second phase.

For now, we were enjoying a quiet day of rest and relaxation.

I had gone with a group of our executives to play golf at the Luana Hills course, a gorgeous location in the midst of a tropical paradise. On the first hole, I hit a great shot off the tee and then hit a good second shot up to the fringe of the green. I was walking from the cart, talking to one of the guys I was with and getting ready to chip my third shot.

Suddenly the earth started moving. I'd never felt anything like it. It was like the world had all at once decided to turn upside down. Vertigo on steroids.

I caught myself with my club to keep from falling. One of the guys with me said, "Hey John, you okay?"

"I don't know," I said. "I feel weird."

After a few moments, I started feeling a little better. Whatever it was, it sort of stabilized itself. I hit my chip shot to within a couple of feet of the hole. As I was walking over to my ball to hit the putt, it happened all over again. Suddenly the earth was tipping and spinning on me.

I gave myself a "gimme" so I'd get a par on the hole, walked back over to the golf cart, and plopped myself down in the seat. Mike Adams, one of our veteran executives, took one look at me and said, "Man, you look awful."

"I think I'm just having bad vertigo or something," I said.

The Luana Hills course is up high in the mountains there. Maybe it was the altitude change from the sea level. I'd been dog tired after the first session of meetings and had gone right in to rest without eating anything. Just before coming out onto the course, I'd grabbed a quick hot dog at the club house. Maybe it was a bad hot dog.

I said, "Let's just go to the next hole and see how I feel."

Then, as we rode the cart down a steep incline toward the next hole, it hit again. Now I was having dry heaves. "Man," I said to Mike. "I need to get back to the front of the course."

Another one of our executive vice presidents, Duane Morrow, was following along with us in another golf cart. I managed to get out of Mike's cart and into Duane's. He gave me a ride back to the front of the course. By the time I got there, I was sweating profusely, my shirt soaked through. There was a doctor there just getting ready to tee off. From the look he gave me, I could tell he thought I was having a heart attack. He had me lie down, covered me with a light blanket, and called an ambulance.

I'd never had much in the way of medical issues. The last time I'd been in the hospital was when I was four years old and had my tonsils out. Sure, I needed to lose some weight, and I wasn't exactly in shape to run a marathon. I had borderline high blood pressure, and my cholesterol wasn't perfect. Growing up Southern, my diet wasn't the best in the world. But all in all, I was doing okay. I really didn't think I was having a heart attack.

They trundled me into the ambulance and whisked me off to a small hospital on the northern shore, more of a clinic, really. They ran some tests and couldn't find a thing wrong with me.

By this time, I was feeling a lot better. Still kind of washed out, but at least I wasn't dizzy. They said it was probably an attack of vertigo, and that I should go back to my hotel room and rest. Duane and I grabbed a cab and headed back to our hotel.

Loveanne was planning to return home to Georgia late the following day after the opening session of the trip's second phase. I described to her what had happened on the golf course, and my brief visit to the clinic, and how they couldn't find anything wrong with me, and that I'd be fine.

She said, "John, you look pale. I think you need to come home with me tomorrow."

I went to bed early that evening. The next morning I woke up still feeling washed out and tired, but I got up anyway, went downstairs to the welcoming session for the second group, and gave a 45-minute talk.

That afternoon, Loveanne and I went off to the airport and boarded our plane home. When we got up to above 10,000 feet I felt like my head was going to explode. It was a pounding headache, like my head had turned into a pressure cooker. The flight attendant gave me some Advil.

When we got on the ground the next morning in Atlanta, I called my office and said, "Dayna, I'm gonna go home and just sleep today. Can you call Dr. Roberts and see if you can set something up for tomorrow?" My doctor was over at Emory Healthcare, a big Atlanta hospital system about an hour and a half from where we live. No way was I going there today. I just needed to lie down and get some rest.

We made it home from the airport, and I had just laid down when the phone rang. Loveanne answered it. A minute later she came into our bedroom and said, "That was Dayna. Dr. Roberts called back and said you really need to come in and let him see you today."

No rest for the weary. Okay . . . I hauled myself back up, put on my shoes, and followed her out the door. We got in the car and drove the 90 minutes back down to Emory, headed inside into the executive center and in to see Dr. Roberts. He ran all sorts of tests, blood work, EKG, checked my balance and motor skills, and everything seemed pretty good.

"I think it may just be vertigo or fatigue," he said. Then he added, "Just do me a favor, though—go get an MRI before you head out."

They sent me over to the lab where they took me through the weirdly space-age process of getting an MRI. You're in a little tube, like an astronaut preparing for lift-off in a seventies sci-fi movie. Then you start hearing a loud rhythmic *Ping! Ping! Ping! Ping!* like they're methodically shooting industrial rivets into you. Once that was all finished, Loveanne and I climbed back into the car and began our trek back north toward Gainesville.

We were about halfway home when I got a call on my cell phone. It was Dr. Roberts.

"John," he asked, "are you still here at the hospital?" He sounded worried. I didn't like that.

"No," I said. "We're already on our way home."

He said, "Well turn around. You need to get back here right away. You've had a stroke."

Loveanne started freaking out. Understandably, she was very upset.

"I'm sure it's just a minor thing," I said, doing my best to reassure her as we pulled off the road, banked a turn, and headed back the way we'd just come. She drove us back to the hospital while I tried to minimize things the whole way in order to ease her mind but was not doing that good a job of it. Meanwhile I kept thinking, "No wonder my head felt like a pressure cooker getting ready to explode." Apparently, that's pretty much what it *was*.

We reached the parking area outside admittance to the emergency department and found a guy waiting for us there with a gurney for me, ready to throw me on my back and roll me in. That was when it hit me: "You know, John, you just might be in a pinch of trouble here."

Next thing I knew, I was on the gurney and inside the emergency department, waiting for someone to come look at me.

Two years earlier, my mom had been at Emory visiting a friend who was staying in this very hospital. My mom was like me. She loved to talk as she walked and didn't always pay a lot of attention to what she was doing or where she was going. As she was leaving the hospital on that visit she tripped, fell on the steps, and broke her hip. She was 80 years old by then and had some health issues that caused her to be on the blood thinner Coumadin. They had to take her off of that so they could operate on her hip. While they were in surgery, an embolism broke loose. She died on the operating table.

As I lay there waiting to be wheeled over to the neurology section, I glanced over toward the door and realized I was looking directly at the step where Mom had fallen and broken her hip. I was lying on a gurney, in the uncertain aftermath of a stroke, staring at the exact spot that killed my mother.

You want to talk about a dark moment.

I figured I had a choice. I could lie there and contemplate the imminent end of my mortal existence. Or I could shine the light of my thoughts' focus in some other direction.

So I thought about my garden.

You Have to Pull the Weeds

Back in 1999, right before Rick and I were put in charge of the company, I had found myself yearning for the quiet and calm of country life. For years, I'd been living on the outskirts of Atlanta and constantly neck-deep in business. Loveanne and I had wanted to get the boys out of the big public school they were in and get them into some place smaller. We'd heard about a small independent school up near the north Georgia mountains in Gainesville, called Lakeview Academy. That sounded perfect to us. In fact, the whole area sounded perfect to us. Finally we decided it was time to do something about it. We bought a beautiful place up in Clermont, just north of Gainesville, with 45 acres of land.

One day, not long after we got the place, I took the boys out and we walked the land together. They were 10 and 12 years old at this point, and the only life they'd ever known was city life.

"Man," I told them, "This is perfect corn land. We're going to plant a cornfield down here, and this fall we're going to have corn. It's going to be unbelievable. I'm going to show you guys how to do that."

We went out on a Saturday to the feed store and bought all the stuff we needed. I had my tiller up there, and we spent all day just toiling out there in the sun. It felt great. We planted about a half-acre cornfield. It was beautiful, black mountain dirt, the rows laid off all nice and neat, just pretty as it could be. The boys were so proud of what we'd done.

I said, "Guys, when we come back in about three weeks, you're going to have corn popping all over the place here. It's gonna be beautiful."

Things were incredibly busy at Primerica, as always. A day or two later I hit the road, back and forth to New York to meet with the executives there then flying around the country doing meetings in other cities. As I said, I'm a three-million-miler on Delta, and this was why. Turned out it was a good six weeks before I could take my two boys and get back up there to that land. When we did, we were *not* greeted by gorgeous neat rows of the most beautiful corn we'd ever seen. No, what we found when we got there was the healthiest field of weeds in North Georgia. We had stinkweeds. We had ragweed. We had golden-rod. We had everything. And down in there somewhere, when we scrabbled down at the bottom of all the weeds, there were a few stubbly, stunted little corn plants.

This happens to me a lot. I've grown crops that could have been on the cover of *Horticulture* magazine—if they'd ever wanted to do a cover story on milkweed.

We like to think of nature as being something nice and orderly and benign. We're kidding ourselves. Nature is wild. Nature doesn't respect any boundaries or follow your plans. It just goes wherever it wants and does whatever it wants.

Anyone who's ever grown a garden knows this. It's easy to *start* a garden. The challenge of getting a garden from a good start to a good finish is that it takes a ton of weeding, watching, and tending—all the stuff most people don't really want to do. The fact is that it's a lot easier to grow weeds than it is to grow flowers and vegetables. Weeds take no effort at all. They spring up without your even planting them. If you want to grow something productive and not just weeds, you can't just poke at it once every six weeks. You've got to be focused on it every single day.

Your mind works exactly the same way.

The natural state of an untended mind is negative, as James Allen pointed out in 1902 in his wonderful classic *As a Man Thinketh*. "A man's mind may be likened to a garden," wrote Allen, "which may be intelligently cultivated or allowed to run wild; but whether cultivated or neglected, it must, and will, bring forth. If no useful seeds are put into it, then an abundance of useless weed seeds will fall therein, and will continue to produce their kind."

That peaceful core doesn't maintain itself. It takes vigilance and constant effort to stay positive.

Left on their own, negative thoughts will sprout up and strangle any successful, positive thoughts you may have planted there, no matter how strong they are. If you want to succeed, you've got to constantly do mental inventory of what's going on in your brain. If you aren't constantly focused on cultivating your edge, if you don't till and weed your brain every day, controlling what you read and what you allow to come into your head, which thoughts you allow to take root and grow and which ones you pull out by the roots and toss to the side, your thinking will run wild and go to the negative. Inside the head of even the most sane, calm, sweet-tempered person there lurks a raging negativity that will start spreading its weeds at every opportunity. The moment you turn your back, they'll take over the garden of your mind.

> Your peaceful core doesn't maintain itself. It takes vigilance and constant effort to stay positive.

I don't know why this is so, but that's how it is. That's *human* nature.

Because of this, positive thinking is not something you can cultivate just by repeating a few affirmations in the mirror while you're getting ready in the morning. It doesn't work just to go to church Sunday morning, hear a few Bible passages, and think, "Hey, I'm good to go for the week." It's not something you can do here and there, now and then. It's not a matter of simply thinking about the right things, but also about not thinking about the wrong things. And of course, you *will* think about the wrong things. Everyone does. So you have to pay attention and be vigilant.

One more thing I've learned about weeds: It's a lot tougher to dig them out once their roots get deep. Not only is it important to pull them, but it's important to pull them early on. If you let them get a foothold, you'll find that when you do get around to pulling them, all you're doing is snapping them off at the ground level. They'll just grow back again.

The exact same thing applies to negative thoughts.

If you want to keep your mind focused on the positive side of life, you need to be down on your knees, hands in the dirt, pulling out all the doubt seeds, worry seeds, criticism seeds, and frustration seeds. You need to do it all day, every day, before those roots grow too deep.

I wasn't very good about keeping up with the weeding of our 45 acres there in north Georgia, but when it came to our business, I was *on* it. In an organization, one of the leader's prime responsibilities is to tend the garden and keep the weeds under control. I took that responsibility extremely seriously.

I've met many business leaders I admire and learn from, but the big heroes and role models of my life tend to be great statesmen. As I've said, I love to read about the lives of men and women who achieved great things during times of struggle and challenge. One of the biggest reasons I so love reading about leaders like Churchill, Jefferson, and Lincoln is that I am inspired by how they managed to keep themselves calm and maintain their equanimity even when everything around them was chaos.

I don't know why this is, but people love to freak out and panic whenever a problem appears. Maybe there's something exciting in the drama of it, or maybe they're genuinely worried. Whatever is the reason, it happens. Those are the times your peaceful core counts most.

Once Rick and I were in charge of running the company, people were coming to me constantly and saying, "John, we've got a disaster on our hands!"

The first thing I would always say is, "Okay, as a result of what's happened, how many people have died?"

The answer, naturally, would invariably be, "Well . . . no one."

"Okay," I'd say, "now that we've established that we don't have a crisis, what is the situation that we're dealing with?"

Most of what people react to as crises, calamities, and disasters are really just *situations*. There's a big difference between a problem and a situation. If writing a check or making some kind of adjustment to what you're doing can fix it, then it's not a problem. It's a situation. If an asteroid hits the earth, I call that a problem. But that doesn't happen too often.

> Most of what people react to as crises, calamities, or disasters are really just *situations*.

Sometimes, of course, you truly are faced with genuine problems. If sales are suddenly crashing and nobody's getting paid, as happened with us in early 1991, that's a problem. The question is: How do you respond? You can panic and wring your hands. Or you can be possibility-focused, taking care to operate always out of the intention to move forward and not get stuck in where you are. Most problems, though, once you look at them with a calm mind, really aren't problems. They're just situations doing what situations always do, which is to constantly change, challenging us to figure out how to change with them.

Although I had to admit, as they wheeled me down the corridor leading to the ICU on that February day in 2006, maybe this particular situation qualified as a *problem*.

Positive Thoughts Change Your Brain

I stayed in the hospital's neurological intensive care unit for the next three days. They weren't telling me all the gory details, but obviously this hadn't been the "little thing" I'd kept assuring Loveanne in our tense car ride that it must be. This had been a big thing.

Shortly after I first landed in the ICU, my son Kyle burst into the room, having just rushed over from Athens. He was going to the University of Georgia at that time. He looked awful, sweating, pale, just a wreck. He ran in and dove on my chest, hugging me. (Sometimes it's nice to know you're loved.) When I saw his face, I realized just how close they all thought they'd come to losing me. I also realized they were right. It *had* been that close.

When they first admitted me, as I would later learn, my brain was swelling badly. There's not a lot of room inside the skull for the brain to swell, and it was starting to push on my brain stem. They were worried that if they couldn't get the swelling under control, the pressure on my brain stem would be sufficient to stop my breathing and other vital functions.

For the first two days, they debated whether to go in with surgery to remove some of the damaged brain tissue in order to create more space for the swelling and give the tissue room to heal. On the third day, just as they were about to go ahead with the procedure, the swelling finally started going down.

This hadn't been a little stroke. It was a major event. In technical terms, I'd had a *dissection* (a flap-like tear) of the vertebral artery, which formed a clot that went to my brain and wiped out most of my cerebellum. Among other functions, your cerebellum is your balance center. No wonder I'd felt the earth heaving and spinning under my feet.

At first they had no idea what state I was in or how bad the damage was. A procession of doctors and nurses kept coming through my room, looking at my chart, talking to me, looking at my chart again, having me touch my nose and do all kinds of basic motor-skill tasks. I guess I passed their tests because after a week I was released and sent home. I was placed on Coumadin (shades of my mom!) to prevent any further clots.

A few days after returning home to Gainesville, Loveanne and I went back down to Emory to see the neurologist who'd attended my case, Dr. Manuel Yepes, to get the lowdown on exactly what had happened, what needed to happen next, and what my prognosis looked like. Dr. Yepes was head of the neurological department there at Emory, a brilliant guy.

He sat us down and started talking.

"The first thing to say is that the brain is inexplicable. We really don't understand what goes on in the brain. In fact, that's one of the major reasons I went into this field in the first place—there's still so much to learn and explore.

"So here's the situation. John, you've had a massive stroke. Yet here you are, walking into my office, standing in front of me, talking to me, doing fine. Nobody looking at you would ever think, 'This is a guy who just had his cerebellum blown out by a major event.'

"Then there are people who have strokes that are so minimal we can barely find them on a CAT scan or MRI, yet they are so badly impaired that they can hardly move. Why does that happen to them? And why do you go through something so massively damaging and come out the other side walking and talking and functioning completely normally?"

He shrugged.

"If you want my clearest answer, you've had a miracle. My physiological answer is this. Here, I'll show you. . . ."

He had me stand up, then close my eyes and try to walk. It felt like he was giving me a DUI test, only with my eyes closed. I took a step and stumbled. Then he had me open my eyes and walk. No problem. As I sat back down, he explained.

"When you had that stroke in Hawaii and lost your gyroscope, your brain evidently rewired itself immediately, and your eyes became your balance. Your brain taught itself how to compensate with a heightened reliance on your sense of vision. Amazing. The term for this is *neuroplasticity*.

"The thing is, the older you are, the less plasticity you have in your brain. If a child has a major injury to his brain, for instance like your stroke, it's highly possible that other parts of his brain will rewire in order to take over the functions of the damaged tissue. The older we get, the more compartmentalized our brain becomes, to the point where if we lose something, well, we've lost it."

He paused, and then said, "Evidently, you have a very child-like brain."

Loveanne started laughing.

She couldn't help herself. I know she'd have loved to say, "Doc, *I* could have told you that!" But she just laughed, and that was enough. It was the first time in a week that I'd heard that sound, and I'll tell you what, it felt good.

Dr. Yepes smiled and went on.

"We don't understand it all. We do know that there are degrees of plasticity in the brain, but other than the age factor, we can't always say just what determines how plastic an individual's brain may be. But we *have* found that a person with a more curious, more positive mind tends to respond far more positively than someone whose mind is habitually negative and doubtful."

So there really was something to all that positive thinking business.

Be the First to Let Go

In college, I did a lot of backpacking and hiked a pretty good piece of the Appalachian Trail, which starts on Springer Mountain up in north Georgia, not far from where we live, and winds more than 2,000 miles all the way up to Mount Katahdin in Maine. Most people just hike a small part of it. My buddies and I would go hiking that trail for two or three weeks at a time. Every year, though, there'll be some people who start out in March and hike all the way up to Maine, usually getting there some time in August because it takes a good five or six months to make the whole trek.

If you're up in this area in March, you'll see the darnedest thing. The first few trail shelters you get to, 10 or 20 miles in, you'll find a whole mess of food, perfectly good food, just sitting there. Why? Because it's all the stuff people realized too late that they should have left behind.

Here's what happens. People pack up all the supplies they can for the big hike, get it loaded in the car, drive up to the start of the trail, drag it all out of the car, and start hiking. Carrying all these pounds on their backs, pretty soon they come to a sobering realization: They brought too much stuff. They're never going to get where they're going with all that junk weighing them down. As much as they want to hang onto it, they realize that if they want to keep going they're just going to have to let go of some of it.

That's what you have to do in your life.

Once you get out of the car and start hiking, you come to the point where you have to get real with yourself. You have to get rid of a lot of the baggage you're holding onto, or you won't be able to go very far. You can't go through life with every grudge you've ever held, everything you're upset about, everything that got done wrong to you, all stuffed into your backpack. You're not going to make it to the top of the mountain or the end of the trail. And grudges get worse with time. You've got to get rid of that junk now so you can keep moving and keep growing.

You want to be a real leader? Be quick to forgive and even quicker to apologize. Even if somebody thinks you did something that hurt them or made them mad and you're sitting there thinking, "What did I do?" just let it go. Say, "I'm sorry. I didn't mean to do that," and move on. Be the first to let go of the garbage.

Worry. Complaint. Criticism. Bitterness. Feuds. Negativity. You don't need them, and they'll only weigh you down. If you're going to hike that trail, you might as well stop right now and leave them all behind at the shelter. Otherwise you just won't be able to go the distance.

Back in 1999 when we moved up to North Georgia, we got a mutt named Rusty. Rusty was a great dog, but he did love to get out there and roam. We'd try to keep him inside our fence, but our property backs up to a dairy farm. The moment Rusty would see his chance for escape, he'd be gone. You could yell for him all you wanted, but it wouldn't make any difference. You could just forget him coming back for a while. We always knew that when he did come back, we'd better have the hose ready. We knew he'd go find the smelliest, most awful mess in the woods, and he'd roll in it and show up back at home covered with it.

> Be quick to forgive and even quicker to apologize.

I don't know why dogs like to roll in a stinky mess. They just do. And human beings are pretty much the same way. They'll run out and find the stinkiest, nastiest, most awful mess out there and roll in it until they're covered with it.

Just look at daytime television.

Over all the years of constant travel, I've developed a habit. When I check into a hotel room, the first thing I do is hang my coat over the television. I know nothing's going to come out of that thing that will influence me in a positive way.

It's not that I want to be ignorant about what's going on in the world. I do keep myself informed, but I do so carefully and selectively. So much of what's passed off as "news" isn't really news. It's just looking at life with a completely negative or sensationalist slant. Why allow my brain to be polluted by all that negativity? Getting angry or upset about it isn't going to contribute to my life in any positive way. All it's going to do is make me bitter, and nothing good comes out of bitterness.

In data processing there's an expression, "Garbage in, garbage out." With the human brain it's the same thing with one critical difference. With your brain, it's *Garbage in, garbage stays in.* You are not a machine, you're a living, breathing organism, and when you allow your brain to be steeped in a bath of bad news, alarmism, pessimism, criticism, rumor, and gossip, it colors your thinking. That stuff doesn't pour out again. It soaks in and starts changing your view of the world. If you sit in front of the television and let garbage pour into your head all day, you end up with a head full of garbage.

In the eighteenth century Thomas Jefferson said, "A man who reads nothing at all is more educated than a man who reads only newspapers." And this is coming from a man who took education just about as seriously as anyone ever has.

Of course, I'm not saying you should live in a vacuum or stick your head in the sand. Jefferson certainly didn't do that.

Obviously, it's important to know what's going on in the world. It's equally important to manage your exposure and the amount of time you allow that stream of negativity to flow into your brain. Don't allow all the noise, all the finger-pointing and screaming, to influence how you see yourself, your world, and your future.

This again is one of the reasons I so love gardening: It keeps me sane. It puts me back in touch with the basics of my life and with how blessed we are to have this earth, this air, this sun. It reconnects me to that peaceful core.

What's more, kneeling in the dirt always reminds me that I'm up here, not down there underneath it. Hey, every day that starts out on the right side of the grass is by definition a good day.

Go On Being You

Since my honorable discharge from the neurological ICU in February 2006, I've been fine. I never had to go to rehab to recover any motor skills. Dr. Yepes didn't give me any big speeches about changing my routine at work, or taking it easy, or taking on less responsibility. "Let's work on managing your blood pressure and cholesterol," he said. "But, other than that, John, you need to just keep doing what you're doing. Don't start acting old. Just go on being you."

Just go on being you.

Now, I had to think about just what that meant. There's nothing like waking up in the ICU with wires running out of you all over the place, surrounded by beeping machines and nurses with long faces, to make you take a fresh look at your priorities. A situation like that tends to focus the thoughts and prompt a little soul searching.

In another year I would be turning 50. I don't subscribe to any of that nonsense about getting old. I'd always believed that you truly are as young as you feel. Now I had neurological proof of it. Still, there's something about the number 50 that prods a person to do a different kind of self-reflection. At least that's how it was for me. Fifty is halfway through a century. Just the fact alone that I was approaching that number would have probably made me start thinking about the arc of my life a little differently at this point. Throw into the mix a life-threatening stroke, and I was staring deep into the mirror.

Let me tell you what we've all got in common: 100 years from now, 100 percent mortality. I often say this in my speeches. "Live every day like it's your last. One of these days you're going to be right."

Realizing that I'd just nearly died made me step back and take a look at my life. I went through a period of asking myself what I really wanted to do. Did I want to keep doing this all, maybe see if I could shoot for *four*-million-miler? Did I want to slow down? Did I want to retire?

Was that what *go on being you* meant? I didn't think so.

We'd weathered the crisis when Art left. We'd been through that challenging decade of transition in the nineties and made it into the new century. Rick and I had been in a position to help the company flourish as part of Citigroup, and it had done exactly that for years. Could it be that my work here, or whatever work I had to do here that was truly important, was more or less done?

At the time, Citigroup stock was doing awesome, trading for $50-something a share. Rick and I had been well paid in stock options through all those years. I could retire right then with millions in net worth.

I gave it serious thought. Maybe I should just call it a day, turn the job over to someone fresh, and get the stress off my back. Stepping down on the eve of my fiftieth birthday, with millions in excellent stock options, would mean Loveanne and I

would be set for life. We could live in the peaceful country style
we loved. I could garden during the day, read about my heroes
Jefferson and Lincoln and Churchill in the evenings. We could
travel and see all our friends. Heck, maybe I could even show
up at company events now and then as a sort of elder statesman.
The point was that I could let go of all the stress. The brass ring
at the end of the merry-go-round was mine for the grabbing.

I'd be lying if I said I wasn't tempted. But I couldn't do it. If
I did, I wouldn't be true to myself.

I wouldn't be *going on being me.*

The thing was that this wasn't just about my own mortality.
Going through that stroke and my three-day VIP tour of the ER
and ICU also got me to look at the *company's* mortality with a
sober eye.

Yes, Rick and I had had a tremendous run in the six years
since we had taken over. It would have been easy to lull myself
into a false sense of security, to let myself be content with the
idea that Primerica would just go on coasting and growing forever, no problem. But just because denial feels good doesn't
make it a good strategy.

The truth was that there was a situation brewing in New
York that was profoundly affecting our lives at Primerica. No,
I take that back—not a situation: a *problem.* And it was getting
worse. Tempting as it was, I couldn't bail, not just yet. I had to
stay and help guide the company through one more transition.

As it turned out, I had no idea what I was getting myself into.
If I'd thought the nineties had been tough, as the song goes: *You
ain't seen nuthin' yet.*

I was about to head into the most difficult, stressful years of
my life.

PRACTICE #6

Develop a Peaceful Core

To be effective in the world, you have to carry within you a core of untroubled calm, a sense of inner peace that is content in who you are, with all your best intentions and all your imperfections. When you maintain that peaceful core within you, you can weather whatever storms are happening on the outside.

- It takes vigilance and constant effort to stay positive. Tend the garden of your thoughts. Check in with your inner dialog. Pay attention to what you're paying attention to. When you find critical, resentful, blaming, worrying, or complaining thoughts starting to sprout, yank them out and toss them over your shoulder.

- Don't let yourself react to problems with panic or anxiety. Stay possibility-focused. Most problems are really just *situations* waiting for your measured response.

- Be quick to forgive and even quicker to apologize. Grudges only get worse with time. Let go of the garbage.

- Be conscious of how much negativity you're letting into your brain, from television, newspapers, gossip, and so forth. Manage your exposure. Do what you need to do to stay positive, and be protective of your peaceful core.

ACTION STEP

Identify what action you can take every day, or at least every few days, that keeps you calm and connects you with your peaceful core. Write it down. Now write it into your calendar. Don't leave it in limbo. Make it a regular habit to schedule time for that activity. It may be the most important appointment you have.

CHAPTER 7

Decision

Be a Lighthouse

I felt as if I were walking with destiny and that all my past life had been but a preparation for this hour and for this trial.

—WINSTON CHURCHILL

On the roof of our country house up here in Clermont, we've got a cupola with a big rooster weathervane jutting up on top. When the wind blows, that thing spins around like crazy. On the coast, not too far from where we live, there's an old lighthouse. When the wind blows, that lighthouse doesn't budge. It just sits there like the rock it's built into.

Weathervane. Lighthouse. I've made it my business to know which is which, and to never forget the difference, not even for a day.

Most "leaders" are weathervanes. Whichever way the wind blows, that's the way they turn. That just doesn't work. If you want to accomplish something great, something real and effective, you've got to be that lighthouse. You've got to be embedded in the rock. When times are hard and things get ugly, you've got to be that person others look to and see only strength. The one people look to and know they don't have to wonder where you stand.

I believe one of our country's deepest problems is that we have a lot of leaders who change their minds like they change their underwear. Change jobs, change marriages, change friends, change convictions. The problem with the "If it isn't perfect today, I'm gone" attitude is that you never have the chance to apply your efforts and give them the time they need to compound. Greatness doesn't happen in a day, or a week. It's the result of growth and maturation, and that can only happen over the course of time and committed constancy.

> If you're a leader, you can't afford the indulgence of having moods.

I've seen companies where the leadership was so volatile, people would arrive to work in the morning and say, "What kind of mood is he in today?" That's a company that has to fight just to stay standing, even when there aren't big challenges coming from the outside. I've seen it happen, many times, and it's incredibly destructive to the organization.

You can see this sometimes just walking into a store or restaurant. The employees are edgy, irritable, sullen, or tentative. When you see that, I guarantee there's a manager, owner, or someone else they're all looking up to, who is throwing them all off kilter with his or her moods.

We all have our good days and bad days. I understand that. It happens to me too. We may have challenges in our personal lives. Something's happening at home, our child has a problem in school, something upsetting is happening in our neighborhood, we've got an especially troubling hangnail. Whatever. Let me tell you a hard truth. It doesn't matter. If you're a leader, you can't afford the indulgence of having moods. You've got to be the one who, when people come to work in the morning, they already know exactly where you stand. You have to be the one they can count on. You have to be their rock.

By the summer of 2007, my ability to serve as a lighthouse for our company had been tested for years. Before long it would be under full-out assault.

Sometimes It's Brightest Before the Storm

In August of 2007, we held our most amazing convention to date, packing the Georgia Dome to near-capacity with some 35,000 people. It was an electric, magical moment, both for the company and for me. The company was turning 30 ("Year Thirty" was a big theme at that convention) and, as it happened, I had just turned 50.

Great things were happening at Primerica. Rick and I had had a tremendous run for the past seven years. When we first took over in 2000, the company was paying out a little more than $400 million in compensation to reps. By 2006, compensation to reps had grown to $631 million. In mid-2007, it was approaching $700 million. In all my speeches at the time, the big goal was to hit $1 billion in annual compensation by the year 2010. Compared to the struggles of the nineties, it was like we were in a perfect little world, almost like a fairy tale.

At this convention we recognized Bob Safford, that wonderful field leader who'd been so encouraging to me that day back in those difficult times in the early nineties when I gave my first real motivational talk to a hotel room full of leaders. We recognized him because his personal income had hit the $4 million mark. I don't mean cumulative: that's $4 million over a single 12-month period. We also recognized Mike Sharpe, who had hit $5 million. From the field's perspective, things had never been better. Cash to the field was at record levels. So were growth in recruiting and growth in sales. Citigroup stock, which many of our field and home office leaders were heavily invested in, was doing great. And having the prestigious name Citigroup associated with their business was a huge positive.

As we celebrated our thirtieth year and made bold pronouncements for the future, we introduced some new features in the business, for example, a lower-cost ($99) licensing fee, making the business more accessible to more people, along with significant product improvements, which were a huge hit. I've been to a lot of events at the Georgia Dome, and I'd never seen or felt a higher energy level. I thought the roof might come off.

To the casual observer, it would have seemed like things were rock-solid and invincibly healthy in the world of Primerica. Indeed everything looked just about as rosy as it possibly could, even to 99.9 percent of the people *within* the world of Primerica.

But it wasn't.

The truth was that we were suffocating under an increasingly oppressive blanket of regulation and bank bureaucracy that was threatening to strangle us. Although hardly a soul in that stadium knew it at the time, and wouldn't know it for years yet to come, Rick and I had been working for months in a confidential and excruciatingly complicated effort to get Primerica completely out from under the Citigroup umbrella, before it snuffed the life out of us.

You've heard the expression, "It's always darkest before the dawn." True enough, but there's another truth too. Sometimes it's brightest before the storm. And when the storm comes, you can't let it catch you off guard. As important as it is to stay positive, don't ever confuse optimism with naïveté. Be prepared. Know exactly where you stand because it could be sorely challenged by high winds at any time.

Have you ever seen one of those beautiful, balmy afternoons where the sun is shining and everything is peaceful, and then out of nowhere the wind suddenly picks up and clouds appear, and moments later you're in the midst of a full-blown thunderstorm? That's where we were in the sunny days of August 2007.

Stand Firm

When Rick and I first took over as co-CEOs in 2000, the situation couldn't have been better. Even though we were technically a division of Citigroup, we operated with a good deal of autonomy. Sandy Weill, Marge Magner, Bob Lipp, and the other people up in New York knew the two of us well. They respected and trusted us. Besides, they were so caught up in all the issues involved with the integration of Citibank and Travelers. They were up to their elbows in alligators and just as happy not to have our "little" (relative to Citigroup, anyway) Atlanta company take up too much of their attention. We would go up to Manhattan once a quarter and do a review of our numbers with them. Other than that, they pretty much left us alone to run things the way we wanted.

In the years since 9/11, the business environment around us had changed. Within months after the towers had come down, the nation was watching Kenneth Lay being led away in handcuffs on CNN. The collapse of Enron redefined the dimensions of corporate catastrophe, which would soon be eclipsed by the WorldCom bankruptcy. In the summer of 2002, Sarbanes-Oxley was passed. It was a whole new regulatory climate, and as part of Citigroup we found ourselves right smack in the middle of it all.

Sandy had operated each of his divisions as a standalone business, which I believe was a very good strategy. His business model was heavily focused on acquisition. The basic playbook went like this: Acquire a good brand that's having some challenges, straighten up the balance sheet, integrate it, and take the profits to the bottom line. He and his team had built a gigantic company doing exactly that. They were masters at it.

Now, that all changed. Citigroup had grown so huge that every regulator had them in their bull's-eye. Suddenly the regulators were telling Citigroup they couldn't do any more acquisitions until they consolidated the way they ran things. They had to put all their businesses onto common platforms—compliance, operations, financials, legal, and so on. Citigroup was moving all their IT to India, all their phone support to South Dakota, and in general dismantling individual business units and folding things into different pieces of Citigroup. Most of these businesses were banks and investment banking businesses, and this homogenizing process worked fine for them.

For us, it would have been deadly.

None of this stuff related to us. We weren't a bank. Operating under the Primerica name and all the growth and change we'd gone through over the years, we were still essentially A.L. Williams. Rick and I both knew that if we let them start disassembling Primerica and feeding off bits and pieces of it into some larger bureaucracy, we'd be letting them destroy it. Primerica, as we knew it, would never survive the dismemberment.

For example, at one point the directive came down that Citigroup was going to have their bank auditors audit local offices of our sales force. This would have been a disaster. These were small offices, rented and run by individual agents across the country. Admittedly, Primerica was not something people could run out of their living rooms or home offices. If you're selling financial services, you need to have a real office where you hang out your shingle and the public has access. But still, these weren't big commercial offices with staffs of dozens. They didn't have vaults. Having a bank auditor come in, someone who expected to find them functioning like the corporate offices of a big bank, would have made no sense at all.

In our business, you have to have a customized support system. Of the close to 2,000 employees we had in Duluth, 100 percent of them were focused on the care and feeding of our sales force. That was it. It wasn't like there was anyone working on some other channel. And it has to be that way when you're selling financial products through part-time people. You can't just go hire XYZ insurance company that's used to dealing with full-time independent agents. Our system won't work that way.

Of course, these offices had to be audited. But we had our own auditors, people who knew our business, knew our people, knew how our operation worked, that our people were independent contractors and so forth. They knew how to do their job within the framework of our business. This directive would have replaced them with some anonymous auditors who'd have no idea what our business model was.

We spent six months fighting that battle, and that was just one of many.

The Power of a Clear Decision

By 2005, things had changed dramatically. Sandy had left in 2003. Marge Magner, Bob Lipp, and more or less all the other executives whom we had worked with closely over the years were now gone. Rick and I were spending all our time flying up to New York, dealing with people we hardly knew and who hardly knew us, to get an exception from some new Citigroup policy designed to make the federal regulators happy.

The only way we were able to survive was because of our relationship with Chuck Prince, who had replaced Sandy as CEO.

I'd known Chuck well for years. He'd been with Sandy since the early days and had served as general counsel of Travelers Group back in the nineties, when I was president. Rick and I would go through all these back-and-forths with people in the executive hierarchy, and then eventually when we reached an impasse, I would call Chuck. Fortunately, because of that connection, we were able to prevail in every instance where it really mattered.

Still, it was a constant strain. While we had a great connection with Chuck, our relationships with the rest of the executives were, to put it kindly, growing frayed. One Citi executive said we were being "obstructionist," "unwilling to try new things," and told Rick that Primerica was "a subpar business" and "not up to Citigroup standards." One day in a meeting this same gentleman said, "John, you guys need to get your business on the Citi superhighway."

"Look," I replied. "We're an off-road vehicle. They don't do that well on highways."

He didn't think that was very funny. It wasn't supposed to be funny. It was true. We didn't fit into the Citi picture anymore, and this wasn't just a matter of culture clash. We represented fundamentally incompatible business models, and their model, while it was working for them, would kill us if this went on much longer. We were not a big bank with all the accompanying issues they were struggling with.

Toward the end of 2005 (a few months before my stroke), I called Chuck and said, "Chuck, this isn't working. We've got to talk." He came down to Duluth right around the end of December that year with a bunch of his new senior management team, and Rick and I did a whole presentation for them on Primerica.

At the end of the meeting, Chuck said to his team, "Guys, I love this company. These are good people. They do a good thing. We've got to figure out how to allow them to operate within the Citi world without so many restrictions on their style." It was like we had a group hug, shared mugs of hot chocolate, and sat around singing *Kumbaya*. I still refer to this today as "our

Kumbaya meeting." Things got a little better for a little while. Sort of. But not really.

The thing about a big bureaucracy is that just saying something doesn't change anything. We were dealing with armies of auditors, lawyers, and bureaucrats, to say nothing of regulators. By the time I was sitting in Dr. Yepes's office at Emory hearing him do his best to explain why my stroke hadn't completely disabled me, it was clear that no amount of talk or meetings was going to change the situation at Primerica. We just didn't fit into the Citi environment anymore. It was killing us, and putting at risk the financial futures of thousands of people who didn't even know any of this was going on.

Throughout 2006, while I was recovering from the stroke, Rick and I talked the situation over. We both knew we were at a crossroads. Something had to change, or else our business would asphyxiate. We either had to find a way to get Primerica out of Citi, or something really bad was going to happen to our company. And if the two of us didn't do it now, nobody ever would. They're four of the scariest words in the English language: *It's up to you.*

It was time to force a decision.

I love the word *decide*. Here are a few others words that end with the same last four letters: *homicide, suicide, patricide, fratricide.* Here's what *those* words all have in common: Somebody dies. To me, that's what the word *decide* means: the death of all other options.

That's what Rick and I had to do now. It was time to choose a path and kill off all other options.

As I said, I've never been one to write out big ambitious life goals or blueprints. I don't pretend to know what's going to happen 20 or 30 years from now. I just do my best to keep myself focused on the next thing that needs to happen. At that point, there was one thing that had to happen. We had to get out of Citi. *Had* to.

From then on, this single goal would absorb every moment of our time and every ounce of our strength. And it was a good thing it did, because it would take that kind of single-minded focus if we were to have any hope at all of surviving the coming storm.

On September 20, 2006, I flew to New York and had a meeting with Chuck, just the two of us. It was now seven months since that stroke on an Oahu golf course nearly ended my life (or, at least, my life as I had been living it) and set me to deliberating the question of whether to resign or keep going. I'd decided to keep going, and I meant to see this thing through—and see it through right.

"Chuck," I said. "You know and I know that Primerica just doesn't fit in Citibank anymore. The world is changing, and we don't belong here. As I see it, we've got an Option A and an Option B. We can find a way to get us out of Citibank in a positive way, while Rick and I are still around to do it and there's still someone here running the show who we know, someone who knows that our motives are good and that we're not just some yo-yo executives trying to hijack their company. In other words, Chuck, while *you're* still here.

"On the other hand," I said. "I can understand that you might not want to do that. In which case we go to Option B, which is to figure out how I retire. Spending all my time fighting with people over how to run this company is not how I want to live my life.

"One way or the other, I've got to leave Citi. I'd like to leave *with* Primerica, but if that's not possible, I need to negotiate my retirement package."

I had a pretty good sense that he would want me to stay and work on something. At this point, Rick and I had racked up a heck of a performance record. We had managed an excellent relationship with regulators and significantly added to our compliance and control functions. At the same time, we had grown the sales force by 30 percent, boosted insurance sales from 290,000 to 400,000 policies sold (for the first time since 1990), doubled SmartLoans, and grown our investment business. I don't think Chuck gave Option B a second's worth of serious thought. He went right to Option A.

"So," he asked, "Do you and Rick have any ideas on how we would structure a transaction that would work for all parties?"

"Yeah," I said. "We do."

We got Rick on the phone. Rick had all the numbers and all the logistics worked out (of course), and we walked through it all right then and there. Chuck said he would put us together with Citi's mergers and acquisitions team to start the complicated process of preparing to launch Primerica on its own with an initial public offering (IPO).

Ever since, Chuck has referred to that day as our "Moses meeting," because what I was really saying was, "Chuck, let my people go." And he knew me well enough by now to know that if I said we needed to get Primerica out of Citi, I was prepared to do whatever it took to see that goal accomplished. I am an amiable guy, but when I get set on something, I can turn into an immovable object.

After that meeting Rick and I started working with Chuck's mergers and acquisitions team. Neither of us had ever been involved in setting up an IPO before. It's a huge undertaking, incredibly complicated and enormously time-consuming, but we were committed to getting it done, no matter what that involved.

Ironically, our success was part of the challenge. By this time, the big New York banks were having serious issues with their capital ratios. Our business, that is, Primerica itself, was quite capital-rich. We had almost $4 billion in excess capital on the books. Extracting us from the larger company wouldn't be easy.

We worked on this project straight through into the early months of 2007. And man, I don't think either Rick or I had ever worked harder in our lives.

In the spring of 2007, we had to hit the brakes.

As we were in the midst of working on the IPO, Rick and I got a call from Chuck. "Guys," he said, "we have to put this on hold for a few months." He told us they were working on an acquisition of a major brokerage company, Nikko Securities, out of Japan. It was a complicated deal, so our project would have to be back-burnered, but just for the moment. He assured us that when fall came, we would get it all back on track again.

That August, Chuck came down to Atlanta and spoke at that thirtieth-anniversary convention. He told the sales force how much he loved our company, how much he loved Rick and me, and that making sure Primerica was protected would always be foremost in his mind.

"Citi will do the right thing by Primerica," he said from the stage, and tens of thousands of Primerica reps applauded like crazy. Among the 35,000 people packed into that stadium, there were only a handful who knew just how much those few words really meant to us at the time, how many battles Rick and I had fought behind closed doors, and how much we had relied on Chuck to help us weather every one of those storms.

But nobody, not even Rick and I, knew the extent of the typhoon-force winds that were on their way.

Persevere

On October 29, 1941, Churchill paid a visit to the Harrow School in London, which he had attended as a boy. He had at this point been prime minister for nearly a year and a half, and his country was steeped in the horrors of war. Pearl Harbor hadn't happened yet, and the United States was still a neutral force. It was a dire time indeed. During that visit the prime minister made an impromptu speech to the students, which included perhaps his best-known line:

"Never give in, never give in, never, never, never—in nothing, great or small, large or petty—never give in except to convictions of honor and good sense. Never yield to force; never yield to the apparently overwhelming might of the enemy."

As I look at the world today, I see so many leaders, whether in the corporate world or political world, who want to be a lighthouse when the weather's fine and things are going great, but who suddenly turn back into weathervanes the moment things get bad, pivoting to follow whichever way the wind blows. Whether it's a politician following the polls or a businessperson following the trends, they let the extraordinary stress of stormy circumstances determine what their actions are going to be, rather than letting their actions be determined by what is the right thing to do.

That isn't how leadership works—at least, not real leadership. Extraordinary circumstances are *exactly* when rock-solid consistency matters most.

Nobody needs a lighthouse when it's bright and sunny out. A lighthouse is there to illuminate the course when darkness threatens to prevail. Without the lighthouse, nobody could see where to go. That's what leaders do. They make the course clear to everyone. Leaders aren't there to give orders or boss people around. Anyone can give directions and tell other people what to do. A leader's function is to illuminate the way when it's dark and dangerous out there.

> Extraordinary circumstances are *exactly* when rock-solid consistency matters most.

And not just the ordinary dark. Lighthouses *exist* for storms. That's why they're built in the first place: to keep ships from crashing when the weather whips itself into a fury. When there's chaos and trouble. On a beautiful, clear day, when everything is sunny and easy, a lighthouse just stands there looking picturesque. That's great for paintings and postcards. But lighthouses aren't built for calm seas and calm weather. They're there for dangerous and difficult times. That's when they become indispensable because, in those times, without the lighthouse, the organization wouldn't survive the rocks.

It's easy to be positive when everything's great. That's not leadership. Anyone can do that. It's when you're facing tremendous adversity that it's tough to stay focused and clear, yet that is exactly when it's most required, as Rick and I were about to learn.

Chuck was true to his word. When September arrived, he got our project to launch Primerica out of Citigroup cranked up and on the road again. Unfortunately, the timing could not have been worse. Things were starting to go sour in the banking industry, and Citigroup was not doing at all well. Back in April 2007, Citigroup had to cut some 17,000 jobs, letting go about 5 percent of the corporation's workforce. By the fall, the company's stock was slipping badly.

Everything came to a head on Halloween.

An Oppenheimer analyst, named Meredith Whitney, issued a report on October 31 declaring that Citibank was badly undercapitalized and in a precarious position because of the bad mortgage-backed securities on its books. That report made Whitney's reputation. She went from being just another barely known voice in an ocean of financial commentary to being a name and a face. The following year she was featured on the cover of *Fortune*, and CNBC named her Power Player of the Year.

It also *unmade* Citibank's reputation. As Bloomberg put it, "The report hit the stock market with the force of a freight train slamming into a brick wall." The day after the report appeared,

Thursday, November 1, the company's stock plunged. I was watching CNBC that morning and everything was "Citi, Citi, Citi, disaster, disaster, disaster." Rick and I were scheduled to fly to New York that Sunday evening for a meeting with Chuck and his team the next day on the final stages of filing our Form S-1, our official statement of intent to go public. I sent Chuck a quick text: "Are we still on for Monday?"

His text came back: "If I'm still here."

When Monday came, Chuck was gone.

Our principal ally at Citigroup, the one man with whom Rick and I had been able to maintain a strong connection that went back years, the one man who in many ways represented our best hope at finding a solution to our dilemma and a path out of Citi, was out of the picture in the blink of an eye.

What could we do? We could persevere.

We set up a meeting as soon as possible with Gary Crittenden, Citigroup's new CFO. Gary is a very thoughtful, decent guy, and quite brilliant. Despite the fact that Gary was relatively new on the scene, he was the only person we could meet with whom we actually knew.

Citi was in chaos, understandably. It took a few weeks for us to get onto Gary's calendar. For those few weeks, Rick and I were on pins and needles.

When we finally got in to see Gary, we had a presentation prepared, detailing the critical importance of continuing down the path of our IPO. "Gary," we concluded, "we've *got* to get this done. We know things are rough right now at Citi, but we have to make this happen."

He told us he would think it all over and meet with us again soon, which, being a man of his word, he did. We met again a week or two later. He told us it just wasn't going to fly.

"Gentlemen," said Gary. "I'm sorry, but we can't. I completely understand your issues. I get what's going on. But we have huge balance sheet problems right now and with our capital constraints, we can't do an IPO."

It was a real pit-in-your-stomach moment if there ever was one. Fortunately, he wasn't finished yet.

"I'll tell you what, though" he continued. "If you'll work with us on it, help us come up with the right structure and find the right buyer, we could possibly *sell* the company."

Now, we had a whole new conversation.

Do the Right Thing

At this point, the first thing Rick and I had to do was to negotiate a retention agreement for the two of us. Part of the purpose of a retention agreement like this is to answer the question, when you're the CEO and your owners sell the company you're running, what happens to you? You need to have some compensation lined up so the deal makes sense for you.

The truth was, though, we weren't so worried about that part of it. We knew that whatever deal they proposed would be reasonable in that regard. We had a more important agenda regarding how this agreement was worded. We knew that we would be taken care of. We needed to be able to ensure that *the company* would be taken care of.

The only way we would give a thumbs-up to selling the company was if we had a seat at the table. We wanted right of refusal so that, as we explored the range of potential buyers, Rick and I had the power to say, "No, that one's not acceptable."

We got the agreement worked out. Now, we were on to putting together the nuts and bolts of a deal.

All that spring, we worked with a team of investment bankers on the structure of a possible transaction, compiled our list of potential buyers, and began contacting them. By summer, we had filed an offering memorandum and were ready to go.

Citi had rented us the top two floors of one of the most beautiful buildings in Atlanta. We turned them into a Primerica showroom with big displays showing the history of the company, videos playing everywhere, and all kinds of impressive stuff. It was like a luxury auto showroom, only times a hundred. We had a meeting room outfitted with the best audiovisual set-up for our presentations.

That summer, along with Alison Rand, our CFO, general counsel Peter Schneider, and Glenn Williams, our president, Rick and I did presentation after presentation after presentation—to private equity buyers, other insurance companies, anyone who might conceivably be a player in this transaction.

Every big insurance company showed up. There were some huge companies, including all the giants, whom we knew would never work out. We knew that if we stood up on stage and told our sales force, "Hey, guess what, guys, we've been bought by XYZ Gigantic Life," our people would go off the rails. So there were a few companies we didn't even consider. Even so, there were a *lot* of potential buyers.

Meanwhile this was all completely under wraps. Not only did nobody in the field have any idea this was happening, but 99 percent of our employees were also kept in the dark. It had to be that way, both because of insider information constraints and also to not create a panic for the employees at the home office.

Finally, it all came down to two potential buyers.

I'll call the first one Company A. Rick and I thought these guys were strong contenders. We felt confident that they would be a good fit with our people culturally. They were roughly the same size and earnings as us, so it would be more of a merger than a true acquisition. It seemed like it would be a compatible transaction. Even though they would need a lot of financing from private equity firms and other sources to make the deal happen, we thought it would work.

The other potential buyer, whom I'll call Company B, was a large insurance operation that Citi preferred because they had the financial capability to do the transaction themselves. Basically, they could write a check. But Rick and I felt they would not be nearly as good a fit for the field as Company A. If we went in that direction, it could be the culture wars all over again.

Citi worked hard to convince us to go with Company B. We were under a fair amount of pressure to get on board with this plan. Finally, after we'd been in this process for a while, they held a dinner for us in New York with the executives from that company, followed by an evening of presentations that showed us in detail how great things were going to be. The event was carefully designed to bring Rick and me to the finish line and close the deal. They pulled out all the stops. One part of their presentation illustrated clearly just how much money Rick and I were going to get out of the transaction when the deal was done. If we went with this plan, by the time we had fully transitioned the company over to its new owners, the two of us would be very wealthy individuals. It was all extremely persuasive.

But there was a problem. No matter how well positioned they were, how great the balance sheet looked, Rick and I just didn't think the company would be as good a fit. Having a replay of the kind of cultural disharmony we had suffered back in the early nineties would have been challenging enough. I was worried about an outcome far worse than that. Company B had a big operation out in the Midwest. Once we did the deal, would they start laying off our nearly 2,000 people in Duluth and folding their jobs into the new company's existing operation? I feared the answer was yes. So, Rick and I were going to make a lot of money, and all our old friends and employees were going to end up on the street looking for jobs? Was *that* how this whole saga was going to end?

At one point during this elaborate dinner meeting, Rick turned to me and said, "John, you call the ball. You're the one who knows if this is going to work for the field or not. It's your call."

I thought about my dad.

When my father was in *his* fifties he was a top executive at Fabrics America, formerly the Fulton Bag and Cotton Mill. This was at a time when textile manufacturing all started going overseas and the company started coming under siege. For a good ten years, he fought the good fight, trying everything he could to keep that company afloat and save the livelihoods of all those people he had known for so many years. He never gave in, and he never gave up, not for an instant. In the end, though, it was an unwinnable battle. The company was finally shuttered in 1978. In the late nineties the mill was turned into a loft apartment complex.

After the company closed down, my dad busied himself with a lot of different things. He drove a school bus for a while and then went back to work at the labor department, where he had worked earlier. He and Mom knew they were going to be okay. They'd always been able to save money. For them, it wasn't a complete catastrophe. But there were an awful lot of people who'd worked at Fulton for years, as long as he had, who had it a lot harder. He felt responsible for them. He never spoke about it, but I knew it ate at him.

I was in college when the worst of it was happening, so I was not attuned to the situation enough to appreciate fully what he was going through. At the time, I was more concerned with where the party was that weekend. But I could see the toll it took on him. He felt responsible to the people who worked there and did everything he could to try to save those jobs. In that, he ultimately was not successful. There were big economic and demographic forces at work that were simply beyond any one man's control.

Was that where Rick and I were now?

Were the economic currents that drove this multinational, multibillion-dollar giant—by this time the largest company in the world—forces that were simply beyond our control? I didn't know, but I sure was going to do everything I humanly could to find out.

> You have to *be* the thing that doesn't change, the thing people count on. You have to be the lighthouse built on a foundation of rock.

It was now nearly two years since that "Moses meeting" with Chuck Prince, the meeting that started the process of trying to extract Primerica from its untenable position as part of Citi. During those two years, everything had changed. The financial and regulatory world had changed. The makeup of our parent company had changed the person to whom we reported several times over. Everything about our situation was in constant flux. It was like trying to build a house on a foundation that sat on roller skates.

Here's what I learned during those two years:

Situations are going to change. You better be fluid enough to change with them, but you need to keep your mission and purpose constant. You can't count on anything because everything can change and probably will change. You have to *be* the thing that doesn't change, the thing people count on. You have to be the lighthouse built on a foundation of rock.

When the river branches, the best thing you can do is take the fork that looks like the right one. And this wasn't it.

It was a good thing we had negotiated that contract clause that gave Rick and me veto power. This was the time to exercise that power.

"Guys," I said to our hosts at the end of the evening. "I'm sorry, but we can't do this. No deal."

A Gathering Typhoon

Citigroup was very upset with me, understandably so from their perspective. But they knew that without Rick and me, there was no transaction. Eventually, in the course of further discussions, they ended up conceding the point and agreeing with Rick and me. Working out a deal with Company A really was the wiser path.

That sure didn't mean it was easier, quite the opposite. From the standpoint of financing, the deal with Company A was far more complicated and involved a handful of different private equity firms. It's the kind of deal that can go wrong a thousand ways unless it's structured very carefully and with a good deal of expertise. It took time, but by the end of the summer of 2008, we were ready to go. As part of the deal, Rick and I and Company A's CEO were creating a three-person Office of the Chairman and would continue to run the two companies essentially as two completely separate businesses.

After all the months of struggle and pressure, things had finally come together. In fact, we couldn't have asked for a more perfect situation.

The Company A people flew their jet over, picked up Rick and me, and flew us back to their headquarters to negotiate our personal contracts. We all shook hands on the deal. The mood was extremely upbeat. Grand toasts and bottles of champagne were involved. I was elated.

We were flying down to Charleston that weekend with a bunch of friends to celebrate Loveanne's birthday. As I sat on that jet, cocktail in hand, I thought, *Isn't life awesome!* I had started out in this company at $19,200 a year. Now, a quarter of a century later, I was about to be a part of a gigantic and successful merger. Not bad for a kid from Salem, Georgia.

I was so glad I hadn't stepped down in 2006 after my stroke. The last two years of stress, constant travel, and intense negotiation had all been worth it. Yes, I'd lost a lot of money as Citigroup stock declined. But we now had a deal on the table that was going to net me a great deal of money, enough to guarantee my and Loveanne's future, a future even more solid than I would have had if I'd retired two years earlier. What's more, we had secured a bright future for everyone at Primerica. Rick and I had won, and *we* had won. All of us, all our friends, all of Primerica had won. It was the best of both worlds. It was a genuine triumph.

It was September 12, 2008.

When I landed in Charleston a few hours later, I saw the news: Lehmann Brothers was in trouble. Serious trouble.

The early tremors of a coming earthquake shook all that weekend. The following Monday, September 15, 2008, Lehmann filed for bankruptcy. The biggest financial collapse of our lifetime was under way.

It didn't take more than a few phone calls to confirm the worst. All that private-equity financing that we had so painstakingly lined up to finance the merger had evaporated. The whole thing had unraveled. It was over.

Within those three days, our whole deal had dried up and blown away like so much dust in the wind.

What now? Were all those long months and years of negotiation for naught? Rick and I had never stopped standing firm as a lighthouse, not for a moment. But had the waves finally become just too great for the company to keep from being smashed onto the rocks?

PRACTICE #7

Be a Lighthouse

Most leaders are weathervanes. Whichever way the wind blows, that's the way they point. If you want to accomplish something great, something real, then you've got to be a lighthouse, solid, immovable, embedded in rock.

- Be the person everyone else counts on to stand firm when it matters most. If you're a leader, you can't afford the indulgence of having moods. You've got to be the one who, when people come to work in the morning, they already know exactly where you stand. You have to be their rock.

- It's a leader's job to make decisions. To *decide* means the death of all other options.

- Lighthouses are there for dark times. Anyone can be positive and decisive when times are sunny and everything is going great. It's a leader's job to illuminate the course when it's dark and dangerous out there, when there's chaos and trouble.

- Situations are always going to change. You have to be fluid enough to change with them. But even within the current of constant flux, you have to keep your mission and purpose constant. You have to *be* the thing that doesn't change, the thing people count on. You have to be the lighthouse built on a foundation of rock.

ACTION STEP

In your present work situation, what do you stand for? Write a list of those bedrock principles on which you cannot change your position, no matter what.

CHAPTER 8

The End of the World

Don't Burn Bridges

The supreme quality of leadership is integrity.
—DWIGHT EISENHOWER

F or years, people were taking properties and flipping them for insane profits. The economy was on the upswing, and it looked like nothing could stop this crazy, unprecedented wave of prosperity. . . .

I paced the stage as I talked, feeling the mood of the people in their seats. It was the early dark months of 2009. Talk about times that call for a lighthouse. The country was reeling from its worst economic catastrophe in memory, and our sales force were the walking wounded. There were thousands in the audience, every one of them hanging on my words. If someone had pulled the pin from a grenade, it wouldn't have taken the grenade going off to get these people's attention. Just dropping the pin would've done it.

Then it happened, that thing that nobody thought could happen. The banks all went broke. Suddenly everyone was freaking out. Newspapers were publishing hysterical headlines, declaring the end of banking in America.

Does all this sound familiar?

I paused. Time for the punch line.

But here's the thing. That crisis I'm describing? It happened nearly 200 years ago—before your great-great-grandparents were born.

The year was 1837. Andrew Jackson was president. The Louisiana Purchase had just gone through, and people were speculating like crazy in land out west. They would win a tract in a land lottery, put it on the market, and flip it. And then the banks collapsed and everything went [bad]. And all the newspapers said it was the end of the world.

Of course, it wasn't. You can't believe everything you read.

I believe that to win in life, you have to starve your nightmares and feed your dreams. The biggest battle you've got to win every day is the battle in your mind.

Be careful who you listen to. Be careful who you give the keys to your brain to. Choose your thoughts. Choose your destiny.

These are challenging economic times. Absolutely no doubt about it. My question to you is: What are you going to do about it?

In the winter of 2008–2009, I sure wasn't giving any talks about hitting a billion in annual compensation. The thing on everyone's mind, plain and simple, spoken or unspoken, was *survival.* In times of crisis, people look to their leaders to see how they're reacting. They're asking themselves, "Are we going to be okay?" Just by looking at you they have their answer. If you're the leader you have just one job: You *lead.* That's what these people desperately needed.

You probably think I'm talking about myself here, or about Rick and me. But I'm not. I'm talking about our field leaders. For Primerica, they were the heroes of the economic crisis of 2009.

Earlier I said that "getting it done" always means relying on the talents and skills of others. Let me expand on that point for a moment. Sometimes, "getting it done" means relying on the dedication, strength of character, and boundless good will of others. You never know who is going to turn out to be the crucial connection you suddenly need to count on. Sometimes, "getting it done" is flat-out impossible without the help of people who are under even more duress than you are and whose loyalty or allegiance to you crosses bridges that you better not have burned.

Rick and I were about to find out just how true that was.

Build Good Will in Good Times and Bad

When people are going through hell, talking about how hot it is will only make things worse. During difficult times, people need a leader who keeps them focused on what's possible, not on what's wrong. In early 2009, everyone in the world was already telling our people what a catastrophe everything was. They didn't need me to do that. So my approach was pretty simple: Ramp up the positive message any way I could.

"We've made it through the hailstorm," I'd say. "We might have had our windshield broken, but our car is still moving, and we're still on the road. And there's a lot of people and companies out there that aren't."

At least, that's what I was saying from the stage. Beyond those speeches, there wasn't much else I could do for the sales force. There just wasn't room in my brain. I was doing my best to stay positive and come from that peaceful core inside; doing my best to keep everyone focused on what we could control and not worry about

> During difficult times, people need a leader who keeps them focused on what's possible, not on what's wrong.

what we couldn't. I was doing my best to be the lighthouse in the storm.

But I've got to be honest: I was shaken.

Privately, I was having an enormous struggle to keep my head above water. *Our deal is dead.* The thought kept ricocheting back and forth between my ears. All that work in 2007, all that effort in 2008, all the negotiation, all the presentations, all the cliff-hanging, nail-biting, mind-numbing suspense and disappointments and frustrations and perseverance. . . . It all had turned to sand. On a personal level, Rick and I had both lost millions of dollars in net worth because most of our compensation over the last decade had been in stock that was now close to worthless. On a mission level, this company we'd devoted our lives to building was now tethered to a gigantic banking corporation that was crashing like a NASCAR pileup and looking like it might take us with it.

All I could think about was the fact that our deal had fallen apart and that Rick and I had to find some way to get it back. I was so wound up with the existential dilemma of our deal that there wasn't enough of me left to be of much use to the field.

What kept our sales force from completely falling apart during those dark months wasn't me. It was our senior leadership.

Our field leaders knew what Rick and I were going through. Let me rephrase that. They didn't know *specifically* what we were going through because we couldn't talk about the specifics. But they knew we were going through the struggle of our lives. They knew it had to do with their future and the future of all their people,—and they knew they trusted us. That was all they needed. They would call and say, "Hey, we want to let you know, we're praying for you. If there's anything we can do to help. . . ." And beyond that, they kept on being the leaders they are and protecting us—protecting *us*—from just how bad it was for everyone out there.

When the economic tsunami hit, our people were out there on the beach picking up seashells. With everything collapsing, everyone in the country seeing their houses going underwater, watching their savings vaporize, and worrying about going bankrupt, buying a life insurance policy was not at the top of anyone's to-do list. It was a brutal time to be in the financial services business. When someone's life has suddenly become a financial nightmare, it's hard to sell a dream.

The Citigroup name had gone from being a huge credibility plus to being radioactive.

What made things worse for our senior guys was that for most of them, their net worth was in Citigroup stock too. Some of our top leaders were earning almost as much in Citigroup dividends as they were in their Primerica business. Many more were using their dividends to pay their taxes. At its high point in 2007, Citigroup stock was trading at just over $55 per share. By early 2009, it was at $1 per share. That's *one dollar,* as in, 100 pennies. We had a lot of millionaires, both in the home office and in the sales force, who got wiped out overnight.

To make things worse, our SmartLoans program, by this time a significant chunk of our people's cash flow, was decimated and soon disappeared altogether.

Most people couldn't go through all that and come out the other side still positive, still moving forward. To this day, I don't know how they did it. But they did it. It was the end of the world, and they were still here with us.

We could have titled this book *Surviving and Thriving through Challenge and Change* because over my entire three-decades-plus at Primerica, things were constantly changing—and not just in small ways. During the Art Williams years we were a young, aggressive company with this charismatic leader. Then one day, he was gone and everything was different. Then we were suddenly part of a huge Wall Street firm. Now the world collapsed. In the midst of the catastrophe, we somehow had to carry on the fight to become our own company.

Throughout all that bewildering, challenging current of change, one thing I'd worked at constantly was to get along with others and build relationships. If you want to be a real leader, a leader whose impact has depth and weight, then you need cheerleaders who will always root for you, no matter what.

It wasn't until after the economy collapsed and Citigroup was reeling and on the ropes that I began to realize fully just how many cheerleaders we had, and how critical they would prove to be in our struggle to make it through the storm.

The Greatest Ability Is Likeability

Two weeks after the collapse, Rick and I were in Gary Critten-den's office trying to figure out what we could do. "What are our options here, Gary? We've got to do *something*." Every five minutes, Gary was stepping out of the room to take a call from the then-chairman of the Federal Reserve, Ben Bernanke.

As I look back on it now, I can hardly believe that Gary even agreed to meet with us. The credit markets were frozen, the nation was teetering on the abyss of a depression of colossal proportions, Gary was on the phone with the chairman of the Federal Reserve trying to keep the entire economy from collapsing, and Rick and I were sitting there in Gary's office trying to get him to help us work out how to get Primerica out of Citigroup!

It was incredibly kind of Gary to see us that day, but it was also clear that there was nothing he or anyone else could do for us, at least not at the moment. "Guys," he said, "we're looking at the end of the world here. There aren't going to be any deals happening."

We didn't stay long. We figured Ben Bernanke took precedence.

Over the next few months, Gary and Steve Freiberg, then head of Citi's consumer businesses, negotiated with the two of us to sign a five-year retention agreement that would have us stay and keep Primerica going until such time as a new deal could be worked out. It was a fairly generous agreement. If during this term Primerica was sold, then Rick and I would get paid a pile of money. If there was no sale during that term, then at the end of the five years we would still get the pile of money. "Deal or no deal," was the gist of it, "you still get paid—but meanwhile just please stay and keep this thing running while the world sorts itself out."

In January 2009, Rick and I went up to New York to meet with the Citigroup people and their attorneys to work out some of the final details of this contract. The morning of our meeting, I was on the treadmill at the Omni Berkshire Place Hotel, at 52nd and Madison Avenue, where I was staying. CNBC was on, and every story was about Wells Fargo.

It was a media feeding frenzy.

By this point all the big banks had been propped up with an infusion of emergency federal money. The big story was that Wells Fargo had used some of their TARP money to take their sales force to Las Vegas. CNN was running a video clip, taken from someone's cell phone, of all these guys dancing and partying, and so help me, it did have that feeling of Nero fiddling while Rome burned. "Wells Fargo Boondoggling with Your Tax Money," went the headlines.

"Uh-oh," I thought as I sweated on the treadmill. "This isn't good."

The thing is that our business is based on events. Meetings, conventions, incentive trips, you name it. Live events are the fuel that drives the engine. Not money. *Excitement.* We knew that. That's how we'd taken the company out of the doldrums in 2000 through all these years of such strong growth. But would the Citigroup executives understand that?

For the incentive contest we had run through the second half of 2008, the prize was a trip to the Bahamas this February to stay in the beautiful Atlantis resort. People ran hard for that contest, and our sales numbers were as good as they'd ever been. We'd been on track to do our biggest year yet, at least until the sky fell in. And a lot of them hit their targets. We were planning to host 1,500 couples who had already won, qualified, got their tickets, and were ready to go.

The trip was just two weeks away.

I showered, got dressed, and joined Rick. We walked together over to 399 Park Avenue, the Citigroup building. My stomach was in a knot the whole way there. As soon as I got into the meeting room with Gary and Steve and the lawyers, I could tell from Steve's face that it was trouble. You know how you can just tell when somebody would rather not give you the news they have to give you? That was how he looked.

"The Citigroup board met over the weekend," he started. He looked at me, then looked away again and blurted out the rest of it. "They're cancelling all incentive travel."

Atlantis was off. This trip was two weeks out, and they were yanking it out from under our people's feet. But wait, there's more! Our convention that summer in Atlanta was gone. They were cancelling our convention. For a company like ours, that was suicide.

I flat-out lost it.

"They're *what?* This isn't some taxpayer-funded boondoggle! These people *earned* that trip. Guys, you don't understand what you've done. You've unplugged the refrigerator, and now all the food's gonna spoil!" I was getting worked up. "Well congratulations. What you got on your hands right now is a melting mass of ice. And I'm not gonna stick around here and watch you destroy the company I've been with all these years. I will not participate in the destruction of something I love. I'm out of here!"

I shot up out of my chair, said a few other things my editors won't want me to repeat here, left the room, and headed for the elevator.

Please understand: I *hate* confrontation. Hate it like poison. I will do anything to avoid an unpleasant scene. I was brought up to be a peacemaker by a peacemaker. One of the things I'm proudest of in my career is that throughout the decades at Primerica, even during the rockiest and most difficult times we went through, I never engaged in character assassination, never went on the personal attack, never made the people I negotiated with into enemies.

In fact, I consider being likeable as a paramount leadership quality.

There are leaders who take aggressively decisive action and don't care how many people they upset as they do it, and I have no doubt they get things done. But how long will those accomplishments last? You've probably experienced leaders like this, and you may have heard them say something like, "Hey, I'm not here to win any popularity contests, I'm here to get things done." As if being likeable is somehow a weakness. That couldn't be further from the truth. In my view, *the greatest ability is likeability.*

It isn't that being liked is so important per se. It's that when you're liked by many, it's because you've learned how to get along with many, and getting along with many different kinds of people *is* important. To a leader, it's as important as oxygen. When you need to get things done, especially things that are challenging and that won't necessarily please everyone involved—like those months the previous year when we were debating about whether to go with Company A or Company B, before the world came to an end—your own likeability buys you a lot of patience and time.

People will be willing to do a whole lot more for you if they like you. Yes, it's nice if they respect you. And sure, I suppose it's ego-gratifying if they think you're smart. But when push comes to shove, impressing people doesn't really do much for you. Being liked . . . that will do a lot for you. If you're going in for heart surgery, you don't need the most likeable doctor. You need the best surgeon, period. But if you're doing business with somebody, then the person you like—the one who is persuasive, the one you'd most want to spend time around—is the person you're most likely to choose.

Through all the chaos and change of the nineties, and the insanity of the 2000s, one positive condition I was always able to maintain in our dealings with Primerica's ownership and top executives was that whomever Rick and I were working with, while they might not always agree with me, they generally *liked* me.

But right now? There was just no being nice here.

Cancelling that trip, pulling the rug right out from under these people who had worked so hard to achieve what we'd promised them, these people who had exhibited such incredible, inspiring leadership under such duress and trying circumstances, was a first-class violation of the trust our people had placed in us. This issue was too important for tact and diplomacy. I'd reached the point where likeability was the furthest thing from my mind. Right now, being a lighthouse was the priority. And I was flat-out furious.

> People will be willing to do a whole lot more for you if they like you.

I was done with this meeting—*Finished*, with a capital F.

Moments after blowing out of that conference room, I was freezing while standing on the corner of Park and 54th, on the phone with Dayna, giving her the gist of what had happened. I was asking her to get me on a flight back to Atlanta and trying to hail a cab at the same time when I heard a voice calling my name. I turned back, and there was Rick running toward me with his hand outstretched, holding out his BlackBerry.

"Hang on, Dayna," I said, and then, to Rick, "What? I am *not* going back in there."

Rick stood in front of me, panting from his run to catch me before I was gone and held out the BlackBerry. "John, you need to take this." He put it to my ear.

"John?" said a voice that I immediately recognized and would recognize anywhere and under any circumstances. It was Art Williams.

Rick had called Art and was putting me on the phone with him.

Art was very emotional. "Rick told me what's going on," he said. "I get what you're going through. But listen, John, if you leave, it's all over. Everything, all of it. You guys have got to figure out a way to get the company out of Citigroup. You're the only one who can make it happen. You can't walk away. You've gotta stay in the game."

I heaved a big sigh, told him I guessed he was right but didn't really see how I could do that.

"What exactly did you say to them when you left the room?" he asked. I told him. It wasn't something I'll repeat. Art chuckled, and then said, "Yeah, I've said that a few times too. But look, you gotta figure out a way to apologize to them. Tell them you were just being irrational and you didn't mean it."

After disconnecting the line, I handed the phone back over to Rick and shook my head. "Man," I said, "you know you've reached some kind of point in your life when Art Williams is your voice of calm reason and reconciliation."

We both had to laugh at that one. Here I was, the guy who valued being positive and likeable among his highest values, playing the guy who stomped out of the room. And Art Williams, the man who never backed down from a verbal brawl, was playing the diplomat. Art, reminding *me* that likeability is the greatest ability.

Talk about a role reversal.

It was the only laugh I'd have that day, and it almost hurt to smile, but it was worth it.

You Can't Do It by Yourself

Rick and I went back into the building, went up to the second floor, sat down with Gary and the others, and I apologized for my outburst. "Here's the thing, though," I said. "We're not signing this contract. You can put your lawyers away, Gary. It's just not going to happen."

The contract they had worked out included a significant non-compete clause that would have effectively taken away any bargaining power we had. Yes, we'd get a lot of money, but in a sense we were being paid to be quiet and not make trouble.

"If we sign this thing," I said, "we have no leverage. Right now the only leverage we have is that you guys are scared of what happens if we quit. So here's the deal.

"For right now, we're here—*if* we're all going to work on how to get Primerica out of Citigroup. I know you're telling us it's impossible. But I'm telling you, if your view is that Rick and I are important to the business, we're either going to get this thing done or y'all can go figure out how you want to run Primerica, and Rick and I will go work out what we're doing next with our lives."

I was most definitely flying without a net here. I had absolutely no idea what Rick or I would do if this didn't work.

As always, Gary was calm and gracious. "Okay," he said. "Let us take a little time to think about it, and we'll all get back together on this."

Meanwhile, Rick and I had to break the news to the field.

We set up a conference call with our top field leaders. Once we were all on the line, I said, "Guys, we've just come from meetings with Citigroup in New York. Tomorrow I'm going to be making a very tough announcement. This isn't going to be easy. We need to stay together and keep everyone focused. This is happening because of Citigroup's problems, not our business. We need you to be a positive force now more than ever." Then I told them what it was we would be announcing the following day, and waited to see what they would say.

I had no idea how they were going to react.

Looking back, I think this was the moment when our field leaders first realized just how big the problems were that we were facing. Up to that point, they knew Rick and I were dealing with some big challenges on the corporate level. But they trusted us to handle whatever had to be handled. They were out there wrestling with their own alligators. Nobody had any idea just how bad things truly were on the inside. Even if we could have talked about it (which we couldn't), it certainly wouldn't have served anyone for us to do so. But this was different. Now we *had* to tell them. When we explained that the Bahamas trip had been cancelled, and that the convention—the convention!—had been cancelled as well, I think that was when the full gravity of where we really were hit home.

They were amazing. One of them, a tremendously talented guy and a great leader named Bill Whittle, spoke up. "Listen, John," he said. "You guys do what you need to do—we got your back." And they all started chiming in, telling us that we didn't need to worry about them or the field and that they were with us 100 percent. You could feel the love coming through the phone. It was one of the most moving moments of my life.

That was when I fully understood just who the heroes of this company really were.

There's a great story in the Bible about leadership. (It's in Exodus 17:8–13). Not long after bringing the Israelites across the Red Sea, Moses leads his people into battle. Joshua's in charge of the troops on the ground. Their side is badly outnumbered, and the odds are not looking good. So Moses does something truly fascinating: He climbs up onto a nearby mountaintop with two assistants, finds a spot where he can be seen from the battleground below and holds his hands up in the air.

That's it. Just holds up his hands.

And believe it or not, it works. The sight of him up there, hands outstretched, gives those people on the ground the inspiration and courage to keep fighting, which they do.

But there's a problem. Every time he lowers his hands, Moses sees the tide of battle start turning back the other way. He can't afford to let them drop. He *has* to keep them up there. But eventually he gets played out. His arms are just too tired. So he has those two aides stand on either side and literally prop his arms up in the air. And sure enough: they win that battle.

> Everyone is looking to you for confirmation that, despite the dangers and the difficulty, they *are* going in the right direction and they *will* prevail.

To me, there are two lessons in that story, both of them crucial to leadership. The first is that people are watching you. When times are tough, you can't waver. You cannot afford to waffle, get sloppy, or even put your arms down, not even for a moment, because everyone is looking to you for confirmation that, despite the dangers and the difficulty, they *are* going in the right direction and they *will* prevail. That's the lighthouse lesson of the story.

And the other lesson? You just can't do it by yourself.

One thing for sure: Rick and I couldn't have kept this company going through the darkest days of 2009 without some amazingly dedicated people holding our arms up for us.

The Power of a Personal Relationship

Apparently there were people at Citigroup who actually thought about calling my bluff on my threat that Rick and me would move on if they couldn't work this out. After the two of us left that meeting with Gary, Citigroup's general counsel got in touch with our general counsel, Peter Schneider, and asked Peter, "What happens to Primerica if we just fire John and Rick?" Peter and his associate general counsel, Alexis Ginn, put together a presentation explaining what a catastrophe it would be for Citigroup if they threw us out. Citigroup got so mad at that presentation that they almost fired Peter.

It was a contentious time.

Thankfully, the folks at Citigroup who had our backs, and cooler heads (that is, Gary) prevailed. A few days later, we were called back up to New York to meet again. I was still steaming about the sinking of our Atlantis trip and cancellation of our convention. In fact, I was so mad I wouldn't go over to the Citigroup building. Gary had to come out and meet with Rick and me in the lobby of the Omni Berkshire, where we were staying.

"I understand all the trouble you guys are wrestling with right now," I told Gary. "I really do. And in all honesty, if I were you, I'd probably just fire us. But these are people I love, people

I've been with forever. I can't just sit around quietly and let you guys destroy this business.

"Listen, Primerica isn't at its core about insurance or financial instruments. Those are our products, but what we're really offering people is hope and opportunity. When someone signs up with our company we're telling them, 'You can win here. You can go do something great with your life. We're going to help you succeed.'

"And when you go into *that* business, you've got a huge responsibility. When you are in *that* business, you have to answer to a higher standard because you're not just out there in business for yourself and your stockholders. You've become the steward of other people's dreams. You're holding their lives in your hands. And you'd better be very sure, you'd better be absolutely 100 percent sure, that you are telling them the truth."

I had brought with me a book with all our $100,000 earners in it. I started leafing through it, page by page, telling each person's story, what each one had done before joining Primerica, about their families, and so on.

I said, "Gary, when I'm meeting with you, I'm not representing *our* business. I'm representing *their* businesses—and there are thousands of them. Independent people who built their own deal. We've got nearly a hundred thousand people, and ten thousand of them have been with us for more than 20 years, from back in the A.L. Williams days. They don't care about Citigroup. What they care about . . ."

Suddenly Gary put his hand out and stopped me. "Hang on," he said. "Is there a guy named Gary Bush with your company?"

"Yeah," I said. "He's a national sales director in San Antonio. Great guy, ex-military. I've known him a long time."

Turned out, Gary Crittenden had *known* Gary Bush.

"Gary used to be an army dentist," he told us. "He was one of the most influential people in my life. I had completely forgotten until just now, but when I was at American Express"—Gary had been CFO there before joining Citigroup in 2007—"somebody told me that Gary Bush was with A.L. Williams. It just connected for me . . . that's *you guys*."

In that moment of recognition, something happened. Suddenly Primerica went from being an abstraction to being a flesh-and-blood reality for Gary. Up to this point, he hadn't fully grasped just who these thousands of people were, or what their businesses really meant. But he knew who that *one* person was.

What shifted that meeting was the power of personal relationship.

Gary went silent for a moment, his eyes resting on the book I'd been leafing through. Rick and I didn't say a word, just waited for Gary to go on.

Finally he looked up at me and said, "John, you really are fighting for good people, aren't you?"

"Yeah," I said. "That's exactly what we're doing."

He thought for a few moments. Then he said, "Look. Right now things are a mess here. I'm going to give you my advice. I have no idea where or how this lines up with Citi. This is just me talking.

"If I were the two of you, as strongly as you feel about this, I'd go put a deal together, a transaction with a couple or three alternatives. Then I'd come back here, show us what you have, and tell us, 'Take it or leave it.' But you've got to understand, the odds are very good that the answer will be, 'Leave it.' You've got to be willing to walk. This can't be a bluff on your part."

So that was the plan. Work out a new deal, and put our jobs on the line. Combat drill with live ammo. Okay. So be it.

Gary referred us to a small investment banking outfit, Greenhill & Co., Inc., to help us hammer out a plan for a deal. Working with Greenhill, Rick structured an ingenious arrangement that would allow Citigroup to keep control of the assets of our existing business, but would have them pay us to service it. The economics would work for Primerica and work for Citi, and it would be seamless to our sales force and clients. It was brilliant. We also met with all the private equity people we'd worked with the year before, prior to the collapse.

Once we had all our ducks in a row, we flew out to Gary's ranch in Salt Lake City and brought him a transaction with three alternatives. The one we were recommending had the best economics for Citigroup and was the least favorable for Rick and me.

Gary heard us out, nodded, and said, "I knew that's what you guys would do because I know your character. This is great. You put together exactly what you should have. Well done."

Somehow, with Gary's incredible help, we had found a pathway through the storm, a way out of what seemed like an impossible situation. It was all because of the power of personal relationships.

You Have to Become a Force of Nature

But Gary wasn't quite finished yet with what he had to say.

"This is a good plan," he added. "Now you need to meet with people about it but not with me. I have to let you know—I'm leaving Citi."

Wait—*what?*

Just as Chuck Prince had been throughout the years from 2005 to 2007, for more than a year now Gary had been our lifeline. The relationship with him served as our bridge from the perilous cliffs where we stood to safety on the other side of the chasm. Gary was a brilliant CFO who came to Citigroup too late to fix many of the issues they had. In fact, I believe Citigroup would probably have made it through the whole crisis in a lot better shape if Gary had gotten there even a year or two earlier.

And now Gary was gone too. We were on our own again.

I have to tell you that by this point our quest to get Primerica out of Citigroup was starting to feel an awful lot like an Indiana Jones cliffhanger. Just when we thought we'd got hold of that crystal skull, we'd reach out to pick it up and boulders would start falling on our heads.

Rick and John and the Temple of Doom.

We flew up to New York to meet with James von Moltke, a wonderful human being who was new at Citigroup and had just become head of mergers and acquisitions there. James and Michael Korbat (who was then running Citigroup Holdings and today is CEO of Citigroup) were the two people we needed to work with, now that Gary had left. We hardly knew James, but then, we hardly knew *anyone* who was still left at Citigroup. Honestly, we didn't know what we could really expect to accomplish. We just knew we had to keep trying.

When we sat down with James he said, "I love the structure of your transaction. It's brilliant. But instead of selling it to private equity, why don't we do an IPO?"

Rick and I looked at each other. *Did he just say that?*

"Actually," said Rick, "that's what we'd ideally prefer to do."

And that was that. It was time to resurrect the IPO plan. Once again, we were off and running.

And man, did we run. It was July 2009 when James von Moltke gave us the green light. For the rest of 2009, Rick and I and the rest of our team lived out of suitcases at the Omni Berkshire, a five-minute walk from the Greenhill & Co. office at the Colgate-Palmolive Building on Park Avenue. From the moment I got out of bed in the morning until the moment I switched off my hotel bedside lamp at night, I was working on our deal. I did not have a life, other than getting this deal done.

Every day, after we finished up the day's work over at Greenhill, Rick and I would come back to the bar at the Omni Berkshire. There we would rehash the day and talk over whatever our next steps were. The bartender there, Robert Dore, is a tremendous guy, the quintessential witty, caustic New York bartender. He practically became our personal counselor that year.

That fall, we filed our Form S-1 with the Securities and Exchange Commission, formally announcing our intention to go public.

To file the form, we went to one of the big financial printers. Everything is extremely buttoned up and confidential in these places, almost like you're inside a gigantic lockbox. They ushered Rick and me into a small room filled with computers to do the actual filing. Outside the room, on the other side of a long glass wall, the army of attorneys Citigroup had working with us stood and watched us. These guys had watched Rick and me sweating this thing through for months and understood what was at stake.

There was a button we had to press to put the thing into the computer and make it official. Rick and I pressed the button together. The moment we did, a big cheer erupted on the other side of the wall. All the attorneys had started applauding. It was a good moment.

Still, that initial S-1 was a pretty rough blueprint, and it had an awful lot of blank lines in it. There was a ton of financial and logistical information yet to work out. We spent the next six months doing exactly that.

Finally, by March 2010, we were ready to put on our IPO road show. I really had no idea what an IPO road show was, but I got one fast on-the-job education. It was the most grueling thing I've ever done.

Suddenly we found ourselves doing back-to-back, one-on-one presentations with all the big money people—fund managers from Fidelity, Wellington, T. Rowe Price, and other outfits like that. When we weren't doing that, we were giving standup presentations to one large group or another in a hotel ballroom somewhere on the planet. We bounced back and forth to London, New York, Frankfurt, Boston, Milan, and all over. We gave private presentations to the world's top money managers in 14 cities over the course of 11 days, and more than 65 larger presentations to more than 200 institutional investors in five countries.

As exhausting as it was, it turned out to be well worth every minute of lost sleep and every ounce of jet lag. Out of all these potential investors we met with, 96 percent chose to invest, including eight of the ten largest mutual funds in North America.

> Learn to bite your tongue and practice the three ups: lighten up, grow up, and shut up.

During those long months of our Indiana Jones quest, there were days when we would go out for drinks after a meeting to Robert's bar at the Omni Berkshire, and Rick (and sometimes Robert too) would listen to me scream for a few hours. But what we were pursuing together was too important to let ourselves get too dug into a particular position or point of view. We had to remember where we were trying to go and that even when you're clear where you're going, sometimes that can mean heading down what seem like side alleys on the way there.

If you have no real responsibility, it's easy to call in to the AM talk show and rant about what's wrong with what everyone else is doing. But if you're in a leadership position, if other people depend on you, then you've got to figure out how to get to where things need to go. Sometimes that means you have to learn to bite your tongue and practice the three ups: lighten up, grow up, and shut up.

Because you have to bring others along with you, even if they disagree with you, you have to earn the respect of those on the other side of the table.

At the same time, if Rick and I hadn't been so forceful and fundamentally unyielding in what we were after, it would never have happened. That's something else this whole Indiana Jones quest showed me: If you want to get something serious done, you've got to become a force of nature. You need to have the people on the other side of the table know, without the slightest doubt, that you're going to be fair and honest. But you also need to have them saying to themselves, "Oh, man, if we don't do this, then we're going to have to deal with *him*." If you don't have that, then you're not going to get anything done, at least not the tough things, the things that matter.

You have to be rigid—but flexible in your rigidity.

Life is a collection of contradictions; it doesn't fit neatly into a rulebook. You have to be able to navigate through its complexity. A big part of that is learning to work with people of completely different viewpoints. I hear people talk about "getting everybody on the same page." That sounds nice, but it's not reality. You'll never get everybody on the same page. You're lucky if you can get them in the same *book*.

What you *can* do is treat the other people with respect and make sure they know with crystal clarity just where you will bend and where you won't.

. . . But Don't Burn Your Bridges

In addition to learning the IPO road show ropes in the early months of 2010, we also got an unexpected and dramatic confirmation of how far-reaching the implications of a relationship can be and of how important it is not to burn your bridges.

At one point that spring, we gave a presentation at the incredibly gorgeous New York Palace Hotel on Madison Avenue. This was one of those meetings we did standing up in front of a large group rather than sitting around a conference table. This is actually the way I'm more comfortable doing it. It's like that scene in *Butch Cassidy and the Sundance Kid* where they tell Sundance to shoot and he misses his first target. He says, "Can I move?" and once he's jumping around he makes all these crazy shots and nails every target. "I'm better when I move," he says. That's me. If I have to sit around a table, I'll do okay, but I'm much better if you stick a microphone in my hand and put me up in front of a room.

I led the presentation with an overview, and then Rick talked about the infrastructure and the dynamics of the transaction. Alison went through the financials. Glenn rounded third by explaining our products and what we do for consumers. Then I brought it on home with the emotional close.

There was a man there that day named Ron Baron, of Baron Capital Funds, who happened to work about eight blocks away in the GM building, where Sandy Weill now had his office. Sandy had told Ron about our IPO and encouraged him to check it out. After we were finished, Ron came up to me and said, "In all my years doing this, that was one of the best CEO presentations I've ever heard."

As the meeting was breaking up, one of our investment bankers from Citibank leaned in and said quietly, "It's really good that he liked it. He's a billionaire and has a huge fund."

Ron became one of our biggest investors.

One day near the end of March, just a few days before the IPO was expected to take place, Rick and I went over to the GM building to meet with another investor. There are a lot of mutual funds and top financial guys headquartered in that building. As the two of us walked through the lobby on the way toward the front desk to get checked in, we heard a voice shout, "Boys!"

We turned toward the voice. It was Sandy, beaming from ear to ear.

We walked over and Sandy grabbed us both, one arm around each of us in a big bear hug, and said, "All anyone is talking about is Primerica and how well your IPO is going, and I'm just so proud of you guys." He was very emotional.

That was when it hit me: the reason Ron Baron found his way into our IPO was because of Sandy. And there were others who went to Sandy for his opinion before they would consider signing on because they knew that he had worked with us in the past. Sandy hadn't been involved in Citigroup for years now. He stepped down as CEO in 2003, and left his post as chairman of the board in 2006. It was not an easy parting. But it was clear he felt no ill will at all, at least not toward Rick and me. In fact he had proved to be an enormously helpful force in our whole IPO process.

That wasn't all.

A good number of the investors who looked at us came because of Joe Plumeri's recommendation. When Joe left the company in 1999 he went to work with KKR, a big private equity firm, who put him in as CEO of the Willis Group, KKR's insurance brokerage in London. Joe did great work for them. He took Willis Group public and made a fortune for his investors. These investors all knew that Rick and I used to work for Joe, so when the word went out about our IPO effort they called Joe and said, "What do you think about these two and what they're doing?"

And Joe told them, "Great guys, great management, great company."

One of those investors was Ron Baron.

I thought about how differently it all could have gone.

Sandy and Joe are both men with very strong personalities, and men we'd been associated with under extremely stressful circumstances. It would have been incredibly easy for us to butt heads with Joe while he was CEO and I was president. What would have happened if we had? What if I'd dissed him after he left, the way so many CEOs cut down their predecessors, even if only in private? (Of course there is no such thing as "only in private," because it always gets out.) What if we had handled our disagreements in a way that made Sandy into an enemy? How would things have gone if these investors had asked Joe or Sandy what they thought? What if either one of them had said, "Williams and Addison are two of the biggest ding-dongs I've ever worked with"? We'd likely have a very different scenario playing out now.

It was early 2010 and we were still standing in the wreckage and aftershocks of the 2008–2009 meltdown. There were days—many of them—when the odds looked impossibly stacked against us. But Joe and Sandy were both pulling for us and actively helping our cause.

Without our solid relationships with first Chuck Prince and then Gary Crittenden, we never could have gotten to the point where an IPO was even an option. Without our relationships with people like Sandy and Joe, we likely would not have been able to bring the investors we needed to the table. Without that bond of trust with our incredible field leaders, forged and held over decades of sometimes extreme difficulties, the company wouldn't have been able to survive intact long enough for the deal to finally be ready.

If Rick and I had badly harmed any one of those many relationships, would we have gotten to the point where we were now? We knew the answer to that one.

Why do people burn bridges? Honestly, I think it's mainly to make themselves look good. Is it worth it to build yourself up today by making potential enemies tomorrow?

I've seen leaders who, as they progressed in their career, built up a room full of enemies—people they'd stepped on, taken advantage of, done something wrong to, or just plain bad-mouthed—only to discover that while they were busy getting themselves up onto a pedestal, they had also recruited a whole gang of folks just waiting to knock them off it again.

I've seen leaders who, the more successful they got, the more they stopped caring what anybody else thought and the more disgruntled relationships they left in their path. And then the moment they stumbled—and we all will, and we all do—they had people piling on and doing their happy best to tear them down.

I've seen quite a few leaders who, upon arriving at their leadership positions, proceeded to tear down those who were there before them. New CEOs often do this, so do some politicians right after winning their elections. Maybe they're driven by the need to be right, and to make sure everyone knows they were right and the other guy was wrong. Maybe they don't know how to develop a peaceful core and they simply get carried away by their negative emotions. Maybe they're insecure, and cutting down other people is how they seek to build themselves up. Maybe they can't let go of some behavior they thought wasn't fair and feel compelled to point it out every chance they get by blaming the person they see as responsible.

But here's the thing: Life *isn't* fair, and it doesn't matter whose fault this was or who's to blame for that. What matters is the people you're leading. If you've got a grudge or vendetta, then sit down and write a letter about it, spelling out all your grievances. Then, once you've gotten it all off your chest, tear the letter up into pieces and toss them in the trash. Let it go.

It's not worth it. It's *never* worth it.

You can't succeed on your own. Nobody does. If you want to do something great or build something great, you need people who are rooting for you at every step, not people who are waiting to be first in line to knock the feet out from under you. You want to build up a group of people who are pulling for you, not pulling against you—people who want you to succeed, not who want you to fail. These people are especially important in the dark moments when the odds look worst.

On March 29, 2010, at 6:05 p.m., we filed the final version of our Form S-1 with the SEC. It was official: Our IPO was ready to go.

Still, even filing your final S-1 is not the ultimate go-ahead. It's just the completion of your formal *intent* to go public. There were still misgivings and second thoughts happening at 399 Park Avenue, and the possibility that Citigroup would get cold feet and back down was very real. It was barely a year since the economy had collapsed, and at this point IPOs just were not happening. Citigroup had a lot riding on this. This was their first major initiative after coming through the storm. If they tried to do an IPO and it flopped, it would make them look completely incompetent and be a crippling move for them.

> You want to build up a group of people who are pulling for you, not pulling against you.

Right up to the day the curtain was supposed to go up, it was still an open question. Go, or no go?

Had we actually made it through the typhoon and brought our ship to safe harbor at last? Or were there any more rocks waiting for us as we approached the shore?

PRACTICE #8

Don't Burn Bridges

Every leader faces unique circumstances and a unique group of people. But there's one thing that is always the same, in any and every situation where other people are involved: if you want to succeed in building something real, you need to build relationships—and after you've built them, maintain them.

- Real leadership is never something you can accomplish on your own. Getting the job done means relying on the talents and good will of others, and you never know whose help you'll suddenly need to count on.

- One of the greatest abilities is likeability. For a leader, the ability to get along with many different kinds of people is as important as oxygen. People will be willing to do a lot more for you, and give you more leeway when you need it most, if they not only trust and respect you but also *like* you.

- Earn the respect of those on the other side of the table. Make sure the other guy knows that you're always going to be fair and honest and that he knows with crystal clarity where you will bend and where you *won't*.

- Making enemies is never worth it. You can't succeed on your own, and if you want to do something great, you need people who are rooting for you, not people who are waiting to knock you down. You need people who are cheering for you to succeed, not hoping for you to fail.

ACTION STEP

Make a list of people you've worked with in the past and with whom you may have left your relationship in less than ideal shape. What can you do to go back and mend those bridges that may need repair?

CHAPTER 9

Independence Day

Make Your Parents Proud

> I firmly believe that any man's finest hour, the
> greatest fulfillment of all that he holds dear, is
> that moment when he has worked his heart out
> in a good cause and lies exhausted on the field of
> battle—victorious.
>
> —VINCE LOMBARDI

On the morning of April 1, 2010, the day our IPO was scheduled to run, Rick and I hit the street early. Officials from the
New York Stock Exchange had invited us to join them down in
Lower Manhattan where they were holding a breakfast for us,
to talk about the day and what was going to happen before we
headed out onto the trading floor. Rick and I were staying up at
the Waldorf Astoria hotel in midtown and needed to be down at
the Exchange by 7:00 a.m. The car service met the two of us at
6:15, and we headed downtown. It was still dark out.

Ever since 9/11 the front of the Exchange at 18 Broad Street
has been blocked off. Since we couldn't just drive right up to
the front entrance, our car let us out off to the side, at the corner of Wall and Broad Streets. We started walking down Broad
along the barrier toward the entrance, when we realized what
we were seeing. A crowd of people stood outside the barrier. As
we approached the entrance, they all started cheering. A throng

of local Primerica people, folks from our sales force living in the New York–New Jersey area, had assembled here in the early hours of the morning to commemorate the event with us. Up above them, draped across the six gigantic white marble columns that support the famous pediment crowning the entrance to the largest stock exchange in the world, was a giant banner, 30 feet high and 80 feet long, that said, "PRI listed on NYSE," our name in giant big blue letters, along with our new logo: three rings—one red, one white, one blue, representing our sales force, our clients, and our company.

I broke down and wept. I had to sit down for a moment and collect myself.

Once inside and through security, Rick and I were escorted to the room where the breakfast was being held. We were seated next to Duncan Niederauer, the CEO of the Exchange, and had a fascinating conversation with him and the others around us. It had been more than a year, they explained, since they'd seen any major IPO activity happening there. For them, the fact that there was such great demand for this company that was emerging from one of the nation's troubled banks was a great statement of renewal, optimism, and hope for the future.

"I know you two see this day as a big deal for Primerica," Duncan said to us. "But let me tell you something: It's more than that. It's a big deal for *America*."

That was when it sank in: The fact that we had pulled this thing off was as exciting for them as it was for us.

After the breakfast, they took us down onto the trading floor. Alison Rand, Peter Schneider, Glenn Williams, and the rest of the team who'd been closely involved in the inner workings of the deal were there along with Rick and me. We were introduced to Pete Giacchi, who ran the area of the floor that would be handling the trading in PRI stock. Pete showed us around as the people on the floor prepared for another day of trading. When you see the New York Stock Exchange on television, it's easy to get the impression of the trading floor being this gigantic place. In reality it's not all that big, about on a par with a decent-sized hotel ballroom. The trading floor is where all the "pits" are, something like the booths in a smallish trade show. Although more and more of the actual trading these days happens off the physical floor and via computer, there's still a significant amount that happens the traditional way, and the place was a flurry of activity.

At 9:30, the opening bell sounded: DING-DING-DING-DING-DING . . .

Trading had begun.

But not trading of Primerica stock—not yet.

When we were doing our IPO road show presentations, we told people the stock might open at anywhere between $12 and $14 a share. By March 31, interest in the stock was so strong that Citigroup had decided they could afford to price it higher, so they put it at $15. At least, that was where it started. It sure didn't stay there long.

As the opening bell echoed through the room, a throng of people crowded around our pit, guys in blue smocks, the actual floor traders doing the buying and selling. All those presentations we'd done had generated so much interest in Primerica that the stock was *22 times oversubscribed*, meaning that even before it opened there was enormous demand. There was so much activity, with so many bids coming in and so much demand to make a market, that they couldn't match up buy transactions with prices and reach an equilibrium point.

It took nearly a half hour before our stock finally opened— at $19.15.

Rick and I had been down in the pit for the past hour or so, surrounded by all these people running all over the place. Rick was standing there grappling with all the information whizzing around, working to understand the mechanics of exactly what was happening with the trade. One of these guys, an old trader in his smock, walked up to me, slapped me on the back, and said, "Buddy, I just want to let you know, it's been ugly out here for the past year. I've needed to see something like this for a while. Man, this is *old school*."

Pete looked at me, and he and I both jumped up in the air and smacked our chests into each other. He laughed and said, "I gotta tell ya, John, most CEOs don't jump in the air and do the football chest bump." I couldn't help thinking, *Maybe if they felt the way I do right now, they would.*

I looked up at the illuminated electronic ticker that runs along the walls clear around the Exchange. It said, "JOHN ADDISON AND RICK WILLIAMS CO-CEOS OF PRIMERICA ON THE FLOOR . . . OPENING DAY OF PRIMERICA'S IPO . . ."

I walked over to Rick and grabbed him by the shoulders, pulled him away from what he was doing at the moment, and said, "Rick, look! *Look* at this." I pointed up at the ticker, and then waved my arm to take in the whole view of the floor. "Very few people on earth will ever see this, buddy. This is amazing. You need to quit worrying about the details over there for a minute, man. Drink—this—in."

The rest of the day was mostly a blur.

As we walked around the floor and talked to people, Rick and I were getting a steady stream of congratulatory notes via text and e-mail. An e-mail from Jamie Dimon saying, "Freedom must be sweet." A great e-mail from Sandy. A long and very nice e-mail from Joe Plumeri and another from Pete and Judi Dawkins. One of the most meaningful messages of the day came from a guy named Meir Lewis, who was in investment banking at Citi (he's now with Morgan Stanley) and had been very involved with the process. Meir was in Israel at the time and sent me a note saying he'd written out a prayer of freedom for us and put it up on the Wailing Wall that morning.

Throughout the day, I also talked to reporters from print and television. About 40 minutes before the closing bell, I stood in front of TV cameras for a live interview with Liz Claman on FOX Business.

"And now," I heard her say, "the stock that is absolutely the huge story today: Primerica. The Citigroup spinoff is surging in its IPO debut, after pricing *above* its offering range and then selling more than three million shares *more* than originally planned. Joining me from the New York Stock Exchange, John Addison, the co-CEO of Primerica. Well, this is great news for you guys. . . ."

We talked back and forth about the company and its history, about its values and what it does for families, about its future for more than five minutes. As viewers watched the two of us, the headline on the screen read, PRIMERICA IPO SOARS.

We had invited about 200 of our top earners and their spouses to participate in the day. During the afternoon, they came out onto the floor and joined us. As our names ran across that electronic ticker board on the wall, Mike Sharpe came up to me, grabbed me, and hugged me. "I just want to let you know how proud of you I am," he said. "This couldn't happen to a nicer guy."

I looked at Mike. I knew full well that if it hadn't been for our senior leaders and the skill and sensitivity with which they managed to keep the sales force together during those dark times, none of this would be happening right now. If they had given in to panic during that crazy, chaotic time, if our sales force had started bailing on us and sales had started falling, then pulling off an IPO would have been impossible.

During our road show, ongoing performance was critical. When you're selling a business, what you're selling is future performance, not past performance. You can't sit in a room with potential investors for some of the world's biggest investment companies and say, "Yeah, things aren't going so well right now, but we think they'll go better soon." We'd set out in a lifeboat on very stormy seas, and we'd not only made it to safe harbor, but we'd made it there with everyone still in the boat. If we hadn't, none of us would be standing there on the floor of the New York Stock Exchange.

I hugged Mike back and said, "Back atcha, buddy."

For the past two years, I'd been so task-focused that all I could do was keep my eyes on what I had to do the next day. Now, as I stood there and thought back to a year earlier, to those perilous early months of 2009, the full impact of what we'd done here began to fully sink in.

When the economy started imploding in the fall of 2008, if you had done a statistical probability grid of what would be happening at Primerica in April 2010, a successful IPO would have been right near the bottom of that grid. Or, slightly below the bottom. Somewhere near the top would have been the possibility of our no longer existing at all because at one point, during the worst of it in early 2009, Citigroup seriously considered shutting our entire business down.

For them, this would have been no big stretch at all. In the life insurance business, it happens all the time. You build up a big book of business as far as you think you profitably can go, then shut down all new business, eliminate all administration beyond the bare-bones staff needed to maintain existing policies, and now all your profits just drop straight to the bottom line as those policies stay in force. Suddenly your business is pure cream, like collecting rent on a huge property that's fully paid off. There are lots of companies that buy these so-called "run-off books of business."

For Citi, this must have looked like a very attractive option. At the time things were incredibly difficult for them, and on top of that, Rick and I were also being very difficult (from their perspective, anyway) in our insistence on what we wanted the outcome to be.

So Primerica came to within a hair's breadth of being dismantled and turned into a put-out-to-pasture cash cow. This would have meant goodbye sales force, goodbye employees, goodbye to all of it for us and all the thousands and thousands of people we'd known for all those years.

Instead, here we stood on the NYSE floor as our stock's currents surged over the riverbanks and flooded the plains of our IPO, knowing that our company had finally become its own entity, independent and autonomous and free to thrive unfettered. I thought about Jamie Dimon's e-mail again and shook my head in wonder. Freedom was sweet indeed.

At a few minutes before 4:00, Rick and I climbed up and out onto the little balcony where the bell sits. There's a big button you push that makes the electronic bell do its DING-DING-DING-DING-DING, and a massive gavel you smash down to signal the close of trading.

At 4:00, Rick pushed the button and I smashed down the gavel. Partners as always.

Trading was over. PRI had finished the day at $19.69, up more than 30 percent from its $15 starting price, and we had racked up a total of 24.6 million shares sold.

When we took the company public, its market cap value was about $500 million. As of this writing, it has grown to well in excess of $2 billion. It is a strong and vibrant public company.

Several hundred companies launched IPOs during 2010. When you compare their offering prices and where their stocks are trading five years later, the top-performing company of them all is Tesla Motors, the first American automaker to go public since Ford's IPO in 1956. In second place after Tesla: Primerica.

Our IPO was not just a success. It was a *blazing* success.

Thursday, April 1, 2010, was April Fool's Day for the rest of the country. Not for us. For us, Independence Day came three months early that year.

You're Here for a Reason

During the battle to bring Primerica safely out of Citi, I spent a good deal of time on airplanes and in hotel rooms reading about World War II and the life and times of Winston Churchill. An HBO movie about Churchill and World War II had just come out called *Into the Storm,* starring Brendan Gleeson as Churchill. Delta had an in-seat video service. I would board my plane, get into my seat, and the moment we were up in the air I'd switch on that movie and watch it again. I watched it probably 20 times. Maybe more.

During that time, I carried a Churchill quote everywhere I went: "Strength is granted to us all when we are needed to serve great causes."

Churchill had led a fairly checkered career as a politician. As a young man, he'd been quite a successful politician, but by the time he reached his fifties he was out of favor and out of power. Watching the Nazis rearming Germany, during the twenties and thirties, he told people, "Look, this guy Hitler is not getting ready for a party. He means trouble and we're going to have to deal with it." But the men in power in England at the time didn't want to hear that. They had all fought in the Great War as young men. The last thing they wanted to contemplate was another war with Germany. They called Churchill an alarmist and a warmonger.

When Hitler invaded Poland and England was forced into the war, Churchill's perspective was vindicated. Neville Chamberlain resigned and on May 10, 1940, at the age of 65 and after a decade in the political wilderness, Churchill fulfilled his lifelong dream of becoming prime minister of England.

In an interview conducted many years later, when Churchill was an old man, the reporter asked, if Churchill could live one year over again, which year would he choose? His answer came without hesitation: "1940." That year was by any measure Britain's darkest hour. It was the year Italy and Japan allied themselves with the Germans and France surrendered to them. It was the year before America would enter the war, the year of the Blitz. It was the year of no hope in sight, when Churchill knew it all came down to him and his people against the Nazis.

My answer to the reporter's question would be: 2009.

In Churchill's writings, he describes the day in the middle of that dark year when he first became prime minister:

> I felt as if I were walking with destiny and that all my past life had been but a preparation for this hour and this trial.

That describes perfectly how I felt now.

In the end, it all made sense: answering that little newspaper ad, resigning from Life of Georgia, becoming Art's "numbers guy," being put in charge of compensation, sticking my neck out and speaking up at that "Hindenburg at Lakehurst" meeting, befriending Rick . . . hey, even that massive stroke on the golf course seemed to make sense now, in the big scheme of things. All the events, circumstances, and decisions of decades seemed to have led to this moment, to this point in time.

As I said, I'm no good at writing up big, sweeping life blueprints, but there was a blueprint there, all right. Just because I didn't write it and didn't always understand it, didn't mean it didn't exist or that it wasn't important that I follow it. All those events came to this: save the jobs, livelihoods, and in many cases the dreams of thousands of people.

Obviously, fighting to save a company isn't the same thing as going to war with all of Western civilization hanging in the balance, and I'm not comparing myself to Winston Churchill. The point I'm making is that every one of us, from Churchill to me to you, we each have our destiny.

You're here for a reason.

That brings me back to the reason I'm writing this book in the first place. You may never be the CEO of a company or president or prime minister of a nation at war. Each of us has a different path to walk. But no matter what your path looks like, where it takes you, and what roles it places you in, I know this about your life:

It means something.

You may not know right now exactly what that meaning is in all its glorious details. I didn't have a clue, or at least not much of one, until it started unfolding in front of me. That's all right. You don't necessarily need to know all that. A life is like a good story: Give it time, give it space, do your best to tell it right, and it will all work itself out and reveal itself in good time.

> Live the story you want to tell.

The opportunities will present themselves, the occasions will arise, for the story to take shape.

I was at an airport one day, hustling from one gate to the next, when I noticed a young kid walking with his mom with these words on the back of his T-shirt: LIVE THE STORIES YOU WANT TO TELL. It stopped me in my tracks. I regrouped and headed over toward the mom. "Excuse me," I said. "Look, I'm not being weird here—but would you mind if I took a picture of the back of your son's T-shirt?" I explained that in my line of work, I often give talks to large audiences, and that quote was so great I wanted to use it in my presentations. (Fortunately, she believed me.) I still have the photo and still use the quote.

Live the story you want to tell.

Some people live their whole lives vicariously through the achievements of famous athletes, rock stars, movie stars, and other celebrities. Not that that's entirely a bad thing. As I said, everyone needs heroes. I've certainly got mine. We all need role models to inspire us in our search for the right forks in the path, and in that sense, part of the way you learn to live your truest life is by trying on other people's stories, the stories of those people you most admire.

But how much greater it is to live your *own* story?

Make Your Parents Proud

After trading closed and the Exchange began the process of shutting down for the day, Rick and I were whisked back into a car and driven uptown again, back to the historic Waldorf Astoria, where we had a big event taking place in the magnificent Grand Ballroom.

When I was a little kid, I would stay up late on New Year's Eve with my parents to watch Guy Lombardo and his Royal Canadians in their annual television broadcast. Every year without fail the announcer would say, "From the famous Waldorf Astoria Ballroom in New York. . . ." This evening, I was going to host an event there.

The very first time I'd actually walked into that ballroom was back in the late nineties, when I attending a dinner there. I vividly recalled how intimidating it had all seemed at the time. The Waldorf Astoria Grand Ballroom can seat 1,500 for dinner.

Look up, and you're staring four stories up at a forty-four-foot ceiling. I remembered looking down at the silverware laid out a foot wide on either side of the plate and realizing I had no idea which fork or spoon we were supposed to start with. Next thing I knew, an army of servers was bringing out food I'd never even heard of before. Everyone around me seemed like they knew exactly what to do. To me it felt like a foreign country. It was Day One in Political Science 101 at UGA all over again. I remember thinking, "Oh, man . . . I am *not* ready for this!"

In those days, I used to have a dream. I'd be at Georgia State, in the last day of our final exams, and suddenly realize I'd missed the entire semester. "I'm not ready for my MBA," I'd say. "I am totally unprepared!" Back then, those same fears sometimes invaded my waking hours too. Many were the mornings, in 2000, when I would wake up in my bed in Gainesville with my first thought being, *John, you are the co-CEO of a billion-dollar division of the largest company in the world. You're a country boy from Salem, Georgia. How on earth did you ever find your way into this position?*

Now, a decade later, here we were.

The event at the Waldorf Astoria got under way at 8:00 and was scheduled to go for an hour and a half, all of it carefully planned out, like a mini-convention. Several thousand Primericans filled the ballroom, and we simulcast the event to all our reps' offices across the country so they could share in the celebration and emotional high of the day. Stock officials later told us they'd never seen any other company hold an event of this magnitude. A series of our top field leaders were there to give presentations, and these guys are some of the finest and most entertaining presenters you will ever hear. Kicking the whole thing off, of course, would be Rick and me. Between the two of us, this was my forte, so I would go first. My plan was to talk about this new day dawning for Primerica, and what it meant

for everyone in this room and across the country. My plan was
to talk about freedom.

Standing up there in the Waldorf Astoria ballroom and looking out over the assembled crowd, I thought about my dad in his
glass-walled office out on the middle of the shop room floor at
Fulton Bag and Cotton Mill. I thought about how hard it was on
him that he couldn't save that company and all those employees'
jobs, that no matter what he did, he could not affect the outcome. Rick and I had been extremely lucky. Our company went
through the biggest storm in generations and faced essentially
impossible odds. Yet, through a long series of circumstances that
none of us could have designed or fully predicted, we had been
fortunate enough to find ourselves in a position where we *could*
affect the outcome. And we had done exactly that.

I looked out at the cheering crowd and thought, *This is for
you, Daddy.*

I walked out on stage, thrust both my fists in the air like
William Wallace in *Braveheart*, and yelled, "FREEDOM!" The
packed room responded with a roar of jubilation.

That right there, I would have to say, was one of the greatest
moments of my life.

When I got back to my hotel room that evening after the
event was all over, I found a note the hotel staff had slipped
under my door. It was from Art Williams. Art doesn't e-mail.
He handwrites a note and then either mails it to you or has it
faxed to you. This was a fax. It had come in during the evening
while I'd been at the celebration. It said:

> I was watching you guys on TV today. The day was
> perfect, couldn't have been any better. I am so proud of
> you guys.   —Art

That note meant more to me than just about any other I've
ever received.

I was way too wired up from the day to even think of sleeping. After reading Art's fax, I changed into some more casual clothes and went back out to join a few friends. A handful of us—Loveanne and I, Rick, my friend Stuart Johnson, and a few others, slipped out the side door of the Waldorf and walked down to our old stomping grounds, the bar at the Omni Berkshire, where sure enough our old friend Robert was tending bar. That place had seen quite a lot of drama during the long months of the past two years. Robert was glad to know it had all worked out.

We sat and celebrated quietly together.

Sometimes you'll hear people use this phrase, "It's a matter of principle." In my experience, most of the time when people say that, it turns out it's really a matter of money. But there are times when something really *is* a matter of principle. Those tend to be defining moments in the overall arc of one's life, moments that reveal who you are, or determine who you are becoming, or both.

At several points in the 2008–2009 process, there was a great deal of money on the table. All Rick and I had to do was pick up a pen and sign a piece of paper, and I could go start picking out which plane I wanted. Those moments brought me face to face with the question: Would I take a big enough payoff to risk selling my friends down the river? And you know, it's easy to say you would never, ever, *ever* do that—until they start adding more zeroes after the number. They start piling on those zeroes, and it's amazing how creative people can get at justifying what they've just done. The more zeroes there are, the more likely you're going to hear someone saying, "Look, I didn't *want* to, but I *had* to do it that way. It was the only way it was going to work."

I lay no claims to being any better a person than anyone else. My human frailties and failings are many and sundry. (Just ask Loveanne and all the other people who know me best.) But in those moments I knew that if I took that particular fork in the river and took a deal that would have Rick and me multi-millionaires but left our friends on unemployment, I would have become a wretched, miserable shell of a human being. As much as it might have seemed like "the only way it was going to work," I would never get another good night's sleep because I'd be waking up at 3:00 every morning for the rest of my life, thinking, "What have I done?"

As I said, events shape your life, but it works the other way too. You also shape events. Life moves on the smallest of decisions, and so does destiny. This *is* a hero's journey, and you're the hero. When the call comes, you have to answer.

"But how do I know?" I can almost hear you asking. "How do I know whether to turn right or left, whether or not to answer that ad, take that job, take this action or that one? If the crucial junctures of life can appear so small and inconsequential in the moments they actually happen, how can I know what the right fork in the path to take is?"

I don't have any solid, sure answer for that. I've probably taken as many wrong turns as right ones, and I'm not saying there's no room for mistakes. Life is full of mistakes. You can't live in fear of making the wrong choices. You have to live it courageously and without regrets. When it comes to tough choices, all you can do is your best. But here is a guideline I've always used that may help: *Make your parents proud.*

When I was a kid, nothing made me feel worse than knowing that something I'd done had upset my mom. Her approval, her being proud of me, was one of the biggest forces that drove me. Knowing that the people I looked up to—her and my dad, Uncle A.W. Dalton, and all their friends—thought Johnny was doing a good job was a huge motivator for me. It still is. You can call that "codependent" till you're blue in the face, but I believe it's a healthy thing, maybe one of the healthiest things there is.

What could be better than knowing you made someone you admire proud of you?

For you, it may not be your parents. Not everyone has parents who were as supportive as mine. Some of us grew up surrounded by people who were negative. Whether it's your parents or someone else in your life you care about, whose views and opinions you value, the same principle still works. When I got married, Loveanne became that person for me. Loveanne is one of the people I look up to most in my life. She is not only a sweet, good person, but she's also incredibly smart and very driven. I have always admired her a great deal. Marrying her changed my life, and not only because I now had someone to provide for and someone beyond myself to think about. That was true, but it was more. I wanted to make my wife proud of me.

Maybe you look up to a teacher, a coach, a big brother or sister. Maybe your kids are the people you want to make proud, or your grandkids. Whoever it is, there's someone in your life that you care about.

Make them proud.

Make Your Someday Your Everyday

Years ago, I visited a little island in the Bahamas with some friends. This place was unbelievably beautiful. The people who owned it had always loved to sail. For years they had dreamed of living in the Bahamas. Not only that, they'd dreamed of *owning an island* in the Bahamas. They started a furniture company years earlier, made a fortune, sold the business, and bought this little island. Now they lived an incredible lifestyle.

There was a guest book there. When I opened the book to write my name in it, I saw that a previous guest had written these nine words:

"Most people's somedays become a handful of people's everydays."

Most people live in the land of the someday. "Someday, we're going to take that vacation I've been promising my family forever. . . . Someday, I'm going to learn another language, take up an instrument, start working out and getting into shape, take dancing lessons with my wife or husband, go hiking with my kids. . . . Someday, I'm going to go visit those places I've always wanted to see, read those books I've always wanted to read. . . . Someday, someday, someday, someday . . ." Before they know it, they find themselves lying in a hospital bed, and they've run out of somedays.

For a very small handful of people, their somedays become their everyday. What they've dreamed of doing becomes how they live their lives.

But here's the crucial point: This is not about having the money.

That's one of the ways we deceive ourselves. We'll do it, we say, "when the money is there." But the money is never *there*. That's not how money works. Money doesn't just show up in great excess and say, "Hey, I'm here, what do you want to do with me?" Bold actions don't start with money. Bold actions start with the taken initiative. The financing falls into place only once the thing is in motion. Our somedays don't keep themselves at perpetual arm's length because of the nature of money. It's because of the nature of *someday*.

It's also not about having the time. "I'll do it when I have the time" is just another way we deceive ourselves. The time, like the money, is never just *there*. There will never come the day that you look at your calendar and suddenly realize, "Hey, look, there's a three-week gap here!" In the same way that nature fills a vacuum, human beings fill time. The only way you'll ever do it is to take that bull by the horns and decide to do it.

Then take whatever steps you need to take to put the pieces in place.

As I said earlier, you need to live every day as if it's your last. One of these days you'll be right. You don't know how long you've got. Maybe decades. Or it could all end tomorrow, just like that. Not only do you not know, but also *it doesn't matter.* Tomorrow will take care of itself. The question is: What do you need to do right now to move your story forward?

> Make your someday turn into your everyday.

Set aside the money, clear the time, and make the reservations. Whatever it is, do it. Make your someday turn into your everyday.

Happiness Is a Decision

One day in July 2001 I was on the road, doing a talk, when I got a phone call from one of our executives, Greg Pitts. "John," he said, "the first thing you need to know is, your family is doing great, everyone's fine."

Oh, I thought, *what's the rest of the news?*

"The bad news is," he went on, "you're having a house fire. And it looks bad."

It was bad. Though they never did figure out what started it, they were able to say that it began in the garage. The car exploded. The whole place burst into flames.

Loveanne was home with the boys when it started. She smelled the smoke, thank goodness, and got everyone out safely, including the cats and dogs. Nobody was hurt.

I needed to get home immediately. It was too late at night to catch a commercial flight. Marge Magner managed to get in touch with the aviation division at Citi, and they flew me home on one of Citi's jets. When I arrived, the firemen were still putting out the fire. The house was not a total loss, but more than half of it was gone. I realized that what I now owned was pretty much what I had with me in my carry-on bag.

And you know what? It was okay. Life moved on. We had each other, we had our lives. It was a devastating event, but it also showed us, with terrible and wonderful clarity, what is important, and what is not. As I stood there watching the firemen work on the wreck that had been my home, my first thoughts were not, "My expensive suits are burned! My big-screen TV that I love is gone!" My first thoughts were about our photos of our kids.

Incredibly, they were mostly okay. One area that had burned the worst was the cabinets where we'd stored all the home-movie videos of the boys we'd taken over the years. The videocassettes were covered in smoke and ash, many of them were warped. Yet we were able to salvage most of the footage.

Life is no cakewalk. It will throw you curveballs, pull the rug out from under your best plans, toss you overboard just when you think you're safe and secure. But even when it burns up half your home (or worse), it will often leave you footage you can salvage and a deepened appreciation of what truly matters.

> Money is a decent scoreboard for how well you're managing the practical necessities of life. But it's a terrible measure of how successful *you* are.

It would be disingenuous of me to say, "Money doesn't matter." Of course it matters. Having money is great. I'm a fan. It's important to know you have your basic security and stability handled. Money is a decent scoreboard for how well you're managing the practical necessities of life. But it's a terrible measure of how successful *you* are.

Over the years I've known a lot of titans in business who've had great success in their positions, achievements, and finances, but who are unhappy, tormented people. I've always told myself, "Whatever happens, I don't want to end up like that." If I should live that long, I don't want to be that 75-year-old guy on a Florida golf course with my marriage a disaster, kids who won't talk to me, my life a train wreck, and my dwindling days lonely and miserable.

> The measure of success is how happy you are—not eventually, not someday, but today, right now.

It's easy to say, "When I'm making a lot of money I'll be happy because I won't have to worry about this or worry about that, and I'll have this handled and that handled . . ." That ends up being a circular argument. The truth is: if you aren't already happy, then getting a lot of money isn't going to make you happy. Money doesn't change people, it just amplifies them. It makes you more of what you already are. If you're unhappy, all more money is going to do is amplify that unhappiness.

Money can't become the thing you focus on. If you do a great job as a leader, you'll make decent money. But if you make money your goal, if you start to worship it, it will never last. Money is a great servant, but a terrible god.

So if money is not the measure of success, what is?

To me, the measure of success is how happy you are—not eventually, not someday, but today, right now. If you are putting off happiness until some imagined future condition, I have some bad news and some good news. The bad news: That planned-for happiness will never come. And the good news: Happiness is actually available to you right here, right now. In fact, that is the only place and time it *is* available.

Often people miss the happiest times of their lives, thinking about what it's going to be like *when* . . . when whatever. When this happens, when that happens. When I get more stuff. If stuff made you happy, we'd have a lot more happy people. But happiness isn't the result of more stuff. It's a state that you place yourself in, consciously and intentionally.

The thing so many people don't understand about happiness is that it's not an emotion. It's a decision. It's a state of mind, not a situation. Happiness is not the fruit of success. In fact, it's the other way around. True success is the fruit of personal happiness. Genuine happiness comes from the heart, not from your circumstances.

Back in the early days, when the kids were tiny and Loveanne and I were living in our little ranch house in Snellville with our little garden out back, scrimping to buy our Christmas stuff at Big Lots, we were happy. We're happy today. And we've been happy right through the whole process in between. What has made us happy and kept us happy? Doing the things we love to do, the things we were designed to do best, and with the people we want to do them with.

If you wait for success to make you happy, you'll always be miserable. You can't wait for things to be better to be happy. You've got to be happy first, in order for things to start getting better. And when you are, they will, because happiness attracts people, it draws people to you. When you're truly happy, you become a beacon of positivity in a world of negativity. You become the person that other people want to be around.

I need the basics of life: food, shelter, the essentials handled for my family and me. Our photos of the boys. A garden. Honestly, that all doesn't take that much money. Beyond that, there are lots of things I like, lots of things I enjoy. There's one thing I *need*. I need it to be there when I wake up in the morning, and I need it to be there every day: I need to feel that what I'm doing makes a positive difference in people's lives. To me that feeling is like oxygen. If it's not there, I can't breathe. If it is there, then I'm a happy guy.

Live a Life that Makes a Difference

I set out to write about leadership and in the process I've told you the story of my life. The funny thing about that is that, I don't know that I ever actually set out to *be* a leader. I mean, it wasn't a goal that I consciously or intentionally set for myself. And you know: I'm not sure that's how leadership really happens anyway. I think the leaders we admire most tend to be those people who set out, not so much to become someone who leads, so much as to live a life of service—service to others, service to a cause, service to an ideal.

> The leaders we admire most tend to be those people who set out to live a life of service.

Maybe that's what all these nine "practices" boil down to: nine steps on the path of doing your best to live a life of service.

Decide who you are and keep moving forward. Shine your light on others, build on your strengths, and earn your position. Focus on what you can control, and develop a peaceful core. Be a lighthouse; don't burn bridges. And make your parents proud.

Maybe the key to building real leadership is simply this: *to live a life that makes a difference.*

A trip around the sun is so brief. Benjamin Franklin said, "You may delay, but time will not." The passage of time is inexorable, and it goes by so quickly for every one of us. In this short stay you have here, why not make the trip worthwhile?

One morning in September 2011, the day after we went on television to announce our plans to build a new global headquarters in Duluth, my assistant Dayna greeted me when I arrived at the office by saying, "John, do you know a Gerald Padgett?"

Gerald Padgett. Did I know that name? I sure did. Mr. Padgett was my first boss. He was that vice president at Life of Georgia who took me into his office in 1982 when I announced my resignation and told me I was making the biggest mistake of my career going to work at A.L. Williams.

It was now nearly 30 years later. I figured Mr. Padgett must be, what, in his eighties now? Many years earlier Life of Georgia had been acquired by Internationale Nederlanden Groep (ING), the Dutch banking and financial services giant. In 2005, ING sold the company to Jackson National for its book of business. I knew what that meant: the Life of Georgia policies then in effect became assets for Jackson National to manage, and Life of Georgia folded in upon itself and effectively ceased to exist. It was the same fate that nearly befell Primerica before our IPO.

At one time Life of Georgia had been a major enterprise with its own tower jutting up as a proud part of the Atlanta skyline. Now it was a memory. And at Primerica, the fly-by-night operation that Mr. Padgett had predicted wouldn't last more than a few years at best, now we were building our own tower.

I couldn't help reflecting on the irony of our history. Half the companies that were in the top 100 life insurance firms in the mid-eighties, like Life of Georgia, now no longer existed. Which meant that of all those companies that had made such a ruckus about us, claiming we wouldn't last, every one of them was gone. And little A.L. Williams had grown up to become one of the most successful insurance companies in the nation.

I asked Dayna if Mr. Padgett had left a message. "No," she said. "Actually, he sent a handwritten note."

John—Saw you on TV last night. Very proud of what
you've done. I don't know if you remember when I told
you you were throwing your life away. Thank God you
had the good sense not to listen to me.

Life moves on small decisions.

A year and a half later, on a warm, sunny Friday afternoon
in May 2013, we held our biggest celebration since our IPO: the
much anticipated grand opening of our magnificent new world
headquarters. The governor of Georgia was there to join us,
along with an enormous crowd of Primericans, friends, family,
media, and other locals who had all gathered to be part of the
event. And that wasn't all. Art Williams and his wife, Angela,
were there too. It was quite a full-circle moment.

> Life moves on the smallest
> of decisions.

Our old headquarters, which
we moved to back in 1985 when
I was still just learning the ropes
as director of compensation and
licensing, was housed in ten separate buildings, which was great
but not exactly ideal. This incredible new facility consisted of
a single, three-story building with connecting wings housing
58 conference rooms, a state-of-the-art theatre and adjoining
television studio, a 248-seat café, and an interactive tour called
"Imagine," designed to showcase the new global headquarters to
current and prospective representatives and employees. Covering
more than eight acres, our new home at 1 Primerica Parkway sat
at the hub of the burgeoning Gwinnett County business, sports,
and entertainment community.

Feeling the warmth of the sun on my face, I thought back
to 1985, when we first moved here to Gwinnett County. Back
then this area consisted of a cemetery, a truck stop, and us. We'd
come a long way.

At the ribbon-cutting ceremony, we buried a time capsule containing an assortment of key mementos marking the company's history. It will stay buried there until long after I'm gone—that is, unless I live to be a 120. The date the capsule is schedule to be opened: February 10, 2077, the company's one-hundredth anniversary.

I won't be there to see it, but I can already savor how it'll feel to those who are.

PRACTICE #9

Make Your Parents Proud

Your life means something. Every one of us has our own destiny. Each of us is here for a reason. You may not always know exactly what that reason is or which path to take, but if you do your best to follow it, it will reveal itself in time. And whenever you hit a fork in the path and aren't sure which way to turn, ask yourself this: "Who in my life do I care most about?" And then make them proud.

- Live the story you want to tell. It's important to have heroes whose stories you admire, but how much more exciting is it to live your *own* story. This *is* a hero's journey, and you're the hero.

- Don't wait for the extra money, or the extra time, or the extra opportunity, to put your destiny and your dreams into action. Tomorrow will take care of itself. Take initiative now. Start making your somedays turn into your everydays.

- Don't let money become the goal you focus on. Money is a decent scoreboard for how well you're managing the practical necessities of life, but it's a terrible measure of personal success. If you make money your goal, it will never last.

- Happiness is a decision. Not an emotion, not a situation, not the result of success but the source of success. Genuine happiness comes from your heart, not your circumstances. Find what it is that makes you happy, and make sure you are doing *that*.

ACTION STEP

List the people you care about most in the world. Now ask yourself, what would make them proud of you? And how would that feel?

Epilogue

On April 1, 2015, five years to the day since our triumphant IPO, Rick and I finally stepped down as co-CEOs of Primerica. Our good friend Glenn Williams (no relation to either Art or Rick), who had been with us through thick and thin during those incredibly tough years as the company's president, became the new CEO.

Glenn started out in the sales force at A.L. Williams in 1981 (which means he predates even me!) and became part of the corporate team in 1983, where he rose through the ranks. In 2000, when Rick and I took the CEO chair together, Glenn stepped into the position I'd been holding as president. It was incredible to think about how much had happened in the fifteen years between those two successions.

You might remember, from my story of those difficult years from 2006 through 2010, my mentioning several other key corporate team members along with Glenn, Rick, and myself who were part of that core group giving presentation after presentation to potential buyers and investors. One of these was Peter Schneider, then general counsel. Peter, who'd been with us since 2000, and Alison Rand, our CFO since 2000, were also by our sides on the floor of the New York Stock Exchange for our Independence Day. When Rick and I stepped down and Glenn moved from president to CEO, Peter became our new president.

It was the smoothest, most positive, most carefully prepared and well-executed transition the company had ever made. Everyone, from our home team staff to our sales force to our investors, was happy and excited for us, for our company, and for our future.

Shortly after we announced the transition, I received many letters from our sales force. One letter, from our senior national sales directors Mark and Cathy Marchesani, so moved me that I want to reproduce it here, in part:

Dear John,

Please forgive me, this letter is long overdue. Thank you! Thank you for your leadership and service.

We once shared a golf cart, and I asked you how you were able to stay positive [even during times when things were so difficult]. You taught me a powerful leadership lesson when you replied, "I showed up every day and tried to make things better. I showed up every day and tried to be part of the solution, not part of the problem."

John, I have watched you for 29 years show up and be the answer, the solution, the positive force. Thank you. Thank you for your vision, your inspiration, and your wisdom. Thank you for always making decisions in light of how it impacts the field leaders. Your legacy of saving the company and the impact you've had on thousands of families will last for generations.

I've always believed that Primerica was not just about "buy term and invest the difference." It wasn't just about earning extra money. It's about changing the world and making it a better place to live.

Thank you for [having the] courage and wisdom to pass the baton to the perfect man at the perfect time.

I quote this letter for two reasons. The first is that in a single page, the author pretty well captured all the central points I wanted to make in this book. (It's good to know that the messages I've gotten across in my career are pretty much the ones I was hoping to get across!)

The other reason is because of that last line.

Nothing could make me happier than to know that the people in our company believe we did the right thing in passing the baton to Glenn. Because no matter what you do, what decisions you make and actions you take, no matter how well you lead, there will always come that point when you have to pass it on to someone else. And when it does happen, when you look square in the face of whatever you've been able to accomplish in your life and ask the question, *Will this endure?* The greatest satisfaction you can have is to hear back the answer *Yes.*

There is no real success without successors.

None of us, no matter what our skills or talents or training or background, can do it by ourselves. And when we look out for each other and devote ourselves to making sure we have each other's backs?

Then there's *nothing* we can't accomplish.

The Nine Practices

1. Decide Who You Are
2. Shine Your Light on Others
3. Build on Your Strengths
4. Earn Your Position
5. Focus on What You Can Control
6. Develop a Peaceful Core
7. Be a Lighthouse
8. Don't Burn Bridges
9. Make Your Parents Proud

Index

Connect with John Addison

JohnAddisonLeadership.com

JOIN THE CONVERSATION ONLINE:

 @JohnAddisonGA

 /JohnAddisonLeadership

 /in/JohnAddisonLeadership

20% OFF
your next SUCCESS Store purchase*

Shop store.SUCCESS.com for the best and most-trusted books, CDs, DVDs and digital products for success, inspiration, personal development, leadership, and much more.

Visit **store.SUCCESS.com**
and use the code "REAL20."

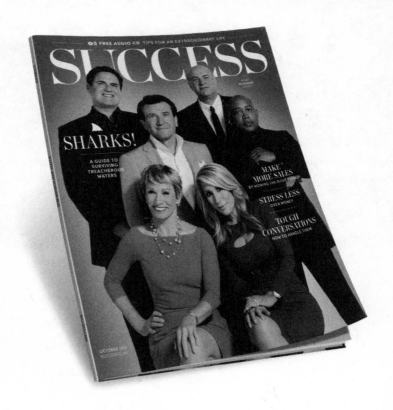

A **GIFT** FOR YOU
1-YEAR
DIGITAL SUBSCRIPTION
TO SUCCESS MAGAZINE

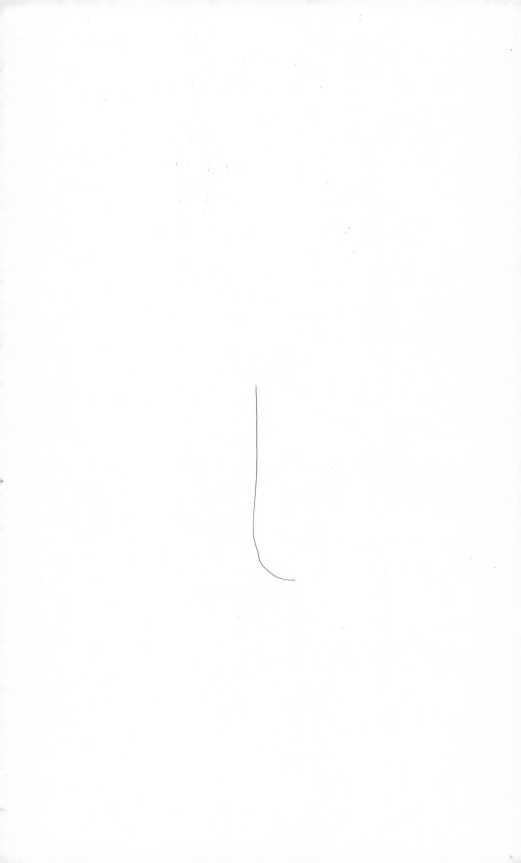